ROAD TRIP

ROAD TRIP

Mark Rozema

Book layout by Elaine Chen
Cover art by Praphat Xavier Fernandes

Library of Congress Cataloging-in-Publication
Rozema, Mark.
  [Poems. Selections]
  Road trip / Mark Rozema.—First edition.
    pages cm
  ISBN 978-1-59709-994-3 (pbk. : alk. paper)
  I. Title.
  PS3618.O935A6 2015
  811'.6—dc23

                    2015006426

The National Endowment for the Arts, the Los Angeles County Arts
Commission, the Los Angeles Department of Cultural Affairs, the Dwight
Stuart Youth Fund, the Pasadena Arts & Culture Commission and the City
of Pasadena Cultural Affairs Division, Sony Pictures Entertainment, and the
Ahmanson Foundation partially support Red Hen Press.

First Edition
Published by Boreal Books
an imprint of Red Hen Press, Pasadena CA
www.borealbooks.org
www.redhen.org

ACKNOWLEDGMENTS

My thanks to the editors of the journals in which these essays first appeared, sometimes in different versions:

Camas: The Nature of the West, "Nurse Log"; *Flyway*, "Rapture"; *Isthmus*, "Make a Joyful Noise"; *Puerto del Sol*, "On the Road to Grand Falls" (first published as "Coming Home"); *Soundings Review*, "Sacred Places"; *Sport Literate*, "The Point of the Game"; *Superstition Review*, "Wherever the Road Goes"; *Weber Studies*, "What Is Not Seen"; and *Written River*, "Three Arizona Canyons."

For the words and the music, thanks: Mary Oliver, William Kittredge, Eddie Vedder, Reggie Watts, Frank Sinatra, Oliver Sacks, George Frideric Handel, Eivør Pálsdóttir, Jim Pepper, James Gleick.

For believing in the book and helping me make it better, thanks to Peggy Shumaker, Kate Gale, Mark E. Cull, Joeth Zucco, and all the folks at Red Hen. Thanks to Xavier for his wonderful photo.

For my father

Contents

Tell me, what else should I have done?
Doesn't everything die at last, and too soon?
Tell me, what is it you plan to do
with your one wild and precious life?

—Mary Oliver

ROAD TRIP

Wherever the Road Goes

Our most necessary preoccupations, obviously, ought to be taking
care of one another, of every other person, and of the sweet world
and discovering the joy of giving part of one's life away. How to proceed is the question.

—William Kittredge, from *The Nature of Generosity*

MY FATHER ASKS, for the fifth time, if we are on Highway 160.
Yes, I tell him. "Why does the road keep changing direction?" he
asks. This too is a question he's asked already. Taking my eye off the
road just long enough to meet his gaze for a consoling moment, I re-
ply, "We're in the mountains, Dad. It's hard to go in a straight line."

My father's eyes are a startling sky blue, the blue of high desert sky on an October day. I'm tempted to describe them as piercing, which is both a cliché and not quite right. They do not pierce,
which is an aggressive verb, and my father is not an aggressive man.
But they do hold one's attention. Until recently, I would say that
those eyes gave the accurate impression of an agile mind at work—
neurons making connections, integrating information, tracing
implications, putting together the pieces of the world. They are
the eyes of someone who wants, always, to understand. I have seen
laughter in his eyes, curiosity, always intelligence and decency—

and never have I seen malice, hatred, or duplicity. Sometimes I still see in those eyes an agile mind at work, but too often now his gaze is watery and lost. I see confusion and panic. I sense misfiring neurons, holes into which my words sink and vanish. It is, increasingly, the gaze of a man entering a fog.

We are crossing the Rockies, and he has been trying to read a road map of Colorado. He doesn't know which way to hold the map, much less make sense of it. The red lines, the blue lines, the numbers and symbols and circles . . . they don't add up to anything that he can discern. This is the man who taught me how to read a map and passed along to me his love of maps. I wonder if he can put it down, give up on the need to have an abstract representation of the landscape, simply look out the window and notice a mountain, a cloud, a red-tailed hawk, a Lombardy poplar bending in the wind. It's not easy for him to do that. He wants, somehow, for the view out the window and the markings on the paper in his lap to converge, to come sharply into focus in a way that is part mathematical equation and part revelation. He wants the map to locate him.

In his hands, the road map is folded into a small square, revealing only the part of the state that we are in. He fiddles with the map, feeling a need to see the whole state, as if that will make all things suddenly clear. "This is no good," he says. "You have to see the whole thing." He can't quite figure out how the map unfolds, and he tears it. "Why do they make them this way?" he says in frustration. Finally he succeeds in unfolding all of Colorado, but the clarity he sought is still elusive. It seems like a trick, this notion that a piece of paper with lines on it might answer the questions "Where am I? How did I get here? Where do I go next?" Staring at the map with those blue eyes, he says, with great tiredness, "Miles and miles of words . . ."

We pass through Mancos, Durango, Bayfield. Every now and then, he has a memory that is uncannily precise. "This is the Piedra River. We camped here in the old white Chevy. Slept in the truck bed." It is as if a brisk wind had cut through the fog in his mind to reveal a blue pocket of sky, a sharp-edged memory, and all the sudden joy that can accompany it. It seems that the names of places bring to him the kind of solace that the map failed to deliver. The amber light of sunset bathes the aspens as we cross Wolf Creek Pass. Names and the stories that go with them are like bright stones at the bottom of a creek. As we pass through the San Juan Mountains, I mention place after place, a litany of lakes in which we fished, forest campgrounds where we pitched our funky old tent-trailer, a little town where the alternator gave out on one of our family trips. I don't know how much he remembers, but I want him to feel that the world is sweet and he is part of it.

We are crossing to the east side of the mountains to seek a new home for my parents. My father's dementia has become too hard for my mother to handle on her own. And so, after more than fifty years in the land of red rocks and twisted junipers, they are moving in order to live near their eldest daughter, in Fort Collins. It's difficult for me to imagine Arizona without them.

My father has driven Highway 160 more times than he could count. Earlier in the day we crossed the Navajo Reservation, where the road elicited from my father no confusion at all. To him—to all of his family—the road from Flagstaff to Cortez is as familiar as a face one sees every day. While it strikes many as a barren emptiness better seen in the rearview mirror, to me it is the landscape of childhood memory, and is therefore beautiful. In particular, the stretch of 160 through Tsegi Canyon always gives me a deep contentment, as if I had slipped into the center of the world. It's a feeling I used to share with my father when we stopped in Tsegi for lunch on hot, dusty summer days, watching slate-blue thunderheads form over Black Mesa, teasing the landscape with the promise of rain.

As a teenager, I used to ride with him in a semi, delivering cases of Pepsi Cola to trading posts and greasy spoons from Gray Mountain to Cameron to Red Lake to Kayenta to Dinnehotso to Baby Rocks to Teec Nos Pos. I loved the days when I could escape the dismal, noisy Pepsi warehouse in Flagstaff, the setting of my first real job, and help him on the reservation circuit. We stopped at all the trading posts. I loved the easy way my father would converse with anyone and everyone, from gruff and hard-headed traders to the skinny Navajo kid on the steps next to a scroungy dog. He moved easily in his skin. I often wondered who, seeing him wheel heavy stacks of soda around and then drive off in his big growling rig, would guess that he was a professor of mathematics. The Pepsi truck was just a summer job.

He does not move easily in his skin anymore. Nor does he converse with ease, even with his wife and children. This morning, as we headed north out of Flagstaff, he stared for a long time at the receding profile of the San Francisco Peaks. On the stretch through Tsegi, he was alert and calm; I hoped he felt the peace he and I used to share in that place. It's hard to know. I wondered if he realized that he would never take this road again. It occurred to me that while I see what he sees, I will never see it quite as he does.

After Tsegi, he dozed. As we neared the junction of 160 and 64, he looked out the window at the scattered hogans and cinderblock houses. Then he turned toward me and emphatically blurted out "Teec Nos Pos." It was clear that I was expected to know why this mattered. "Yes," I replied. "Teec Nos Pos." I searched my mind for the significance of this place, until I remembered it. "Tillie Redhouse lived here," I said. He let that fact sink in as his gaze took in the Carrizo Mountains to the south. "Tillie Redhouse plays the piano," he said, finally, with conviction. He wanted me to know that he still recognized the particulars, the people and places that add up to a life. He wanted to let me know that he was still a participant in the world.

In the years of my growing up, the particulars of my father's work included teaching high school and college, working as a mathematician for the U.S. Geological Survey, serving as a perpetual elder or deacon at our church, driving a Pepsi truck all over the Navajo Nation, and raising five kids. He was a teacher, mentor, elder, father, husband, and coach. The particulars of his surroundings included the Zuni Indian Reservation, with its dusty pueblo and its sacred mountain, the pine-forested town of Flagstaff, Arizona, also with its sacred mountain, and all the wide sweep of land between.

And he was an intrepid explorer with a curious spirit. When I go back to the child's view of the man with whom I grew up, I see, first of all, his smile. I see it as he drives with one sunburned arm out the window. I don't know if anything pleased my father more than a plain red-dirt track into wide open country. It became a family joke, my father's oft-repeated phrase: "I wonder where this road goes . . ." My mother's exasperated response was also a source of amusement to us: "It's just a road, Wes, like any other road. Do we have to know where every road goes?" If he was driving, the answer was yes, apparently we did. His inquiry may have been disingenuous; more often than not, he already had a good idea where the road would go. But why not take it anyway, just to be sure? What better way to spend an afternoon? Why not take a watermelon, a fishing pole, the Coleman stove, a can of Spam, and just see where the road goes?

Wesley James Rozema didn't know where the road would take him when, in 1952, he left his home in Michigan, spurred westward by asthma and a curious spirit. Like so many others in the middle of the twentieth century, he followed Route 66, headed for California with his young wife and two daughters. But there was a lot of country between Michigan and California, and that country laid claim on him. My parents passed the Twin Arrows Trading Post, where a billboard as big as a movie screen proclaimed "See a real live Indian!" In Holbrook, they stayed in a motel of cheesy concrete tipis. Between Gallup and Flagstaff, it seemed he could see forever across the wide sweep of cinder hills, volcanic diatremes, sandstone buttes, dusky blue mountains, and the caliche hills of the Painted Desert. After an unsatisfactory dalliance with California, my folks returned to this land of endless sky and wind and dirt roads, eventually settling in Flagstaff, where my father landed a job at Northern Arizona University as a professor of mathematics.

He might not, while wheeling heavy stacks of pop around a trading post, be easily mistaken for a professor—but then, he was perhaps an unusual professor. I have memories of waiting outside his office for what seemed like hours while he helped students. I recall the day he helped a tearful Navajo girl who protested that she was "too stupid" to do math. I remember how he put her at ease with some chat about places and people. Perhaps when she discovered that he knew who ran the trading post at Chilchinbito, she was surprised and suddenly didn't feel quite as alone at the big university. And before he turned her attention to the equations, he let her know, in a subtle and understated way, that he considered herding a flock of sheep through a labyrinth of canyons and deep sand to be every bit as challenging as mastering differential equations. In short, he treated her as an equal and assumed she was interesting and capable.

My father helped many students who went back to the reservation to become teachers themselves. In the 1970s Northern Arizona University began a concerted effort to prepare primary and secondary teachers to teach in reservation schools. Few math teachers at that time were Native American, and the retention rate for Native students was low. The university wanted to find someone who could effectively prepare primarily Navajo, Hopi, Apache, and Zuni undergrads to become science and math teachers. My father was chosen to direct this program. I know he considers the time spent training these teachers among the most important contributions he has made in his lifetime.

But before he was a professor, he was a high school teacher. In 1955, after determining that the suburbs of Los Angeles were not to his liking, he found his way back to the high desert when a job opened up on the Zuni Reservation, in New Mexico. His job would be to teach mathematics to Zuni teenagers. Back then, the pueblo did not have a paved street, a stop sign, a grocery store, or a hospital. People cooked in outdoor clay ovens. Zuni had few white residents. The preparation my father had for this job was a degree in math with a minor in choral music from a Dutch Calvinist Christian college in Michigan. He had probably never eaten a chili or seen a rattlesnake. To my knowledge, he had no preparation in cross-cultural communication or cultural anthropology. He was a stranger in a strange land.

They put him straight to work. He was a warm body. He taught math, of course, and directed the choir. He also taught health, physical education, earth science, physics, and surely some courses I can't recall. He coached basketball, track, and cross-country. I've seen pictures of a man with a severe flattop brush cut and a whistle standing next to a track team of wiry boys with names like Alvin Owelagte and Estevan Quam. I've listened to a scratchy vinyl recording of his choir singing Handel. I try to imagine his life.

Just as my life began in red dirt, my father's life began in black dirt. I remember him speaking of wading through the black muck of his grandfather's celery farm in Michigan. I barely remember his parents and the wider community of which he was a part—Dutch Calvinists, hard-headed Frisians, ice skaters, and farmers, with names like Veenstra, Rozema. I imagine my father as a teenager reciting the questions and answers to the Heidelberg Catechism. I've seen pictures of him from college, singing in barbershop quartets, playing the double bass. Can I really comprehend the scope of his journey?

The journeys of the generations dovetail. My earliest memory is of playing in the dirt at the Christian Reformed mission in Zuni. Maybe I cried, because some lady who smelled of peppermints scooped me up and brushed me off. I remember also the smell of juniper smoke from the ovens and of sitting in my father's lap, wrapped in a blanket, as we watched from the pueblo rooftop as the procession of dancers entered the plaza. I have written a poem about this, which, like many poems, is a small thread of memory braided with a larger thread of imagination, because, of course, I can't really remember what my four-year-old self thought. The dream is made up, but the feeling from which this poem comes— the clear sense of incarnation and the sense that the Shalako embodied a mystery—was not.

Shalako

Back to the beginning: Zuni, New Mexico,
December, 1966. A four-year-old boy swaddled
in a blanket, sitting on an adobe roof, waiting
for the Shalako. Perched on rooftops
around the plaza, everyone in Zuni waits,
solemn and expectant. Then, out of a whirlwind

of red dust, he emerges, long beak snapping.
Is a man behind the mask? the young boy asks.
Yes and no. God puts on a body.
The shuffle of Kachina dancers in dust, pulse
of rattles and bells, and the constant chanting
lull the boy into a dream: there is no ground
or sky, but only whiteness and he is in it,
floating, as the towering Shalako bends down
low as if to swallow him up, but instead
reaches out and plants a seed in the boy's head.
When he wakes, the boy stares at his tiny hand
as he flexes and unflexes it into a fist.
God puts on a body! Anything can happen.

Like my father wondering about the road ahead, I'm not sure where these reminiscences are leading. Landscape and story, body and spirit intertwined. God puts on a body. Maybe this is true of us all, and not just the Shalako. Old-fashioned Dutch Calvinists are embarrassed by bodies—their hungers, their weaknesses. Bodies lead to sin, bodies age, bodies give out. My father's hands are old, weak now, the skin mottled and papery. They were not always so. A disease is crippling his brain, and this was not always so. Still, the mild man who is my father shines brightly in both body and spirit. Can we see the sacred in the fleeting world?

Here is another story, a truer one than the poem, although the details are fuzzy. My father told me this story many years ago, and I didn't recognize (as young people fail sometimes to recognize) that it was a story that mattered. My father described a conversation he had with a twelve-year-old boy on his track team as they rode together on a long bus trip. They were talking about Zuni religion—always a delicate subject. My father wondered how the Shalako made his wooden beak snap so sharply. Was there a mechanism in the mask? (The twelve-foot-tall Shalako is one of the most beloved and important kachina spirits that inhabit the bodies of men in ceremonial dances. It has a long wooden beak, or clapper, that makes startling noises, perhaps to keep young Zuni children from falling asleep.)

My father was never one to embellish stories. His telling of the tale was sparse, leaving much to speculation. He remembered that the boy hesitated at such an invasive question and stared hard at his coach. I imagine the boy sizing up this white man. (What is he after? Is he making fun of me?) In the boy's hesitation, my father found a way to say to the boy that he meant no disrespect; he understood that the dancer in the Shalako mask was filled with the spirit of the Shalako, and that he was, at the same time, a man. In wondering about how the beak worked, he was merely curious, but he didn't question that a Shalako spirit was involved. The boy was silent for a while. It was not unusual for Zuni kids to be silent. But then he opened up. He told my father, almost apologetically, that he didn't know what made the beak snap. Then he added that he knew it sounded crazy to a white man, but what he and all Zunis believed was that the kachinas came out of the salt lake and entered into the bodies of Zuni men.

In 1955 cultural sensitivity toward Native people was not great, and among white people there was not the widespread respect toward Native spirituality that there is today. The wanna-be tribe was much smaller in number. I don't think Zunis were accustomed to whites being anything but dismissive of their religion. Anthropologists were patronizing, seeing Zuni faith as something to be studied, while missionaries were hostile, seeing Zuni faith as something to be conquered. My father, an evangelical Christian new to the reservation and with no particular insight into Zuni ways, simply saw before him a boy who had entered into an awkward conversation with a white teacher about things that probably ought not to be talked about. My dad assured the boy that it didn't sound crazy at all. He said that his own religion also taught that spirits can inhabit people. And the conversation went no further. One of the things my father understood was when to stop. I don't suppose there was anything remarkable in the content of my father's words, but something in his manner allowed that boy to be both open and vulnerable.

After almost a decade in Zuni, my father moved the family to Arizona, where he finished his master's degree and then became an assistant professor at Northern Arizona University. This was in the days when it was still possible to get such a position without a PhD. In his thirty-five-year career, I think he held the dubious distinction of being the last remaining professor in the Math Department without a PhD. Had he come seeking a job ten years later, he would not have been hired. He didn't often publish in mathematical journals; he had no interest in it. He was a college professor who still believed that teaching was the most important task. He was hired when NAU still wore the old-fashioned label of "Teacher's College."

Throughout my father's life, I have seen in him a willingness to step forward and do whatever needs to be done. In our church, he was a perpetual elder and organizer of projects. He did the work, whatever it was: balancing the finances, painting, roofing the sanctuary, cutting wood for the pastor. And he did the work with a generous spirit, with humility, kindness, and humor. He didn't toot his own horn. In fact, he never thought highly of himself. He considered himself ordinary at best. Growing up under his roof, I thought he was ordinary too. It took a while to discover otherwise.

After he retired from teaching, and well into his seventies, he served on the board of directors for the relief society of his church. In this capacity, he traveled to places like Malawi and Nicaragua, where he worked on projects that involved AIDS and malaria prevention, poverty reduction, microlending, agricultural sustainability, and clean water. In our own country, he went with work teams to areas affected by disasters: flooding in south Texas and California, rebuilding and needs assessment in Louisiana after Hurricane Katrina. In Malawi he caught malaria and nearly died; his stamina was greatly reduced after that. When at age seventy-six he shared with me a slideshow of his trip to Africa, I was struck by his rambling and inarticulate manner; this was new to him. I began to worry.

Five years ago he was hiking the red rocks of Oak Creek with a spring in his step; two years ago he could barely make his legs get him up to the top of the mesa where he could survey the wide sweep of high desert in which he has spent most of his life. He spoke to me, then, of the ways in which I have taught him. He has in the past twenty years read many of the books I send him—especially those with an ecological theme. In response, he said, "I never thought about any of that stuff when I was younger." What he didn't realize is that it all came from him. The love of nature, the love of the world, and the love of people, especially people who are on the margins of society—it all came from him.

Now he is moving into a time of life in which nothing makes sense. The road ahead frightens rather than draws him forward. His logical, linear mind is failing him. He feels that he is a burden to his wife and children. The math teacher no longer balances the checkbook. The driver of big rigs has relinquished his keys.

Light is fading as we drop down the east side of Wolf Creek Pass into the town of Del Norte, where forty years ago the alternator gave out and our family spent the day in a park. He remembers that. To me it was a carefree afternoon to roughhouse with my brother under the locust trees. I didn't worry; cars were grown-up stuff. I didn't know till much later that my dad was flummoxed by car trouble. I didn't know that parents could feel anxiety. What I did know was that I was in my father's care, and that was sufficient.

I am now about the age that my father was on that hot August day in Del Norte. I have children and parents, and responsibility stretches in both directions. I hope that my care is sufficient. We are all in webs of reciprocal relationships, and I know now that the strands connecting us are more tenuous than I once thought. How do we give back to those who have sustained us with love and generosity? The way is not clear, and how to proceed is indeed the question. There is no map that charts the course.

As we leave Del Norte, the last faint glow of sunset slips off the tops of the Sangre de Cristo Mountains. Traveling at night will make my father anxious, so in the next town we will get a motel. He will wake up in the middle of the night, wondering where he is and why everything is strange to him. Nights are the hardest time. He will ask me where we are going, and I will say, as I've said be-

fore, "Fort Collins. A new home." This answer will be of less consequence than what follows: "I'm with you, Dad. Your whole family
is with you." Wherever the road goes.

THE POINT OF THE GAME

As I was putting my daughter to bed one night, she complained of a loose tooth that refused to come out. We discussed various methods of speeding up the process, all of which involved some degree of pain. Not able to find a satisfactory solution, I suggested she run full speed into a wall. "That would do it," I told her. "It worked for me, when I was your age." Never failing to seize an opportunity to lengthen the bedtime ritual, and sensing a story that might afford her the pleasure of laughing at her old man, Angela pressed for details. "It happened when I was just your age," I began. "I was a fast runner in the fifth grade. But I had a friend who was a little bit faster than me. I didn't like coming in second place all the time, so my goal was to beat him in a foot race—just once. Just once, and I would be satisfied . . ."

The abridged version of the story goes like this: I did beat my friend in a foot race, once and only once. I wonder if he remembers this. It was inside the gym at Weitzel Elementary School, in Flagstaff, Arizona, in 1973, in Mr. Riley's PE class. The accomplishment did not give me much satisfaction, but it did relieve me of some teeth. I won the race because my nemesis saw the brick wall and slowed down while I was looking to the side to see who was ahead. By the time I faced forward, it was too late. *BAM.* To everyone's amusement, I spit out two teeth as blood trickled from my mouth. This cautionary tale could mean many things: Pride cometh before a downfall. Watch where you are going. Pay attention, for Christ's sake. Be careful what you wish for. To my daughter, it proved what she already knew: fifth-grade boys are idiots.

From the same period of my life, I have another (and better) memory of running. My family was on a camping trip in northern Minnesota. We had caught a creel of fish, bluegills, I think, at Lake of the Woods, on the Canadian border. It felt like wild country to me, on the edge of some great mystery. We had just finished setting up our tent-trailer (the kind no one has anymore, essentially an aluminum box with a side-flap that served as a kitchen counter) when the sky turned a strange pea-green-soup color and the wind started raking trees at the campground. Tornado weather. My mother, listening to the radio for any reports of funnel clouds, mentioned that the nearby town of Warroad was clocking gusts at seventy-five miles an hour. I remember this because she used the phrase "hurricane force." Our tent would not stay up. We had to eat our Spam and beans and then sleep in the station wagon, which rocked back and forth.

The roiling clouds shifted from shades of charcoal gray to olive green to deep cold blue and seemed to form pockets from which bursts of glorious violence emanated. Lightning shredded the sky above the lake. But there was no place else for us to go. There was only one road to the campground, and it headed back the way we had come, into worse weather. We hunkered down. But no funnel cloud developed, and it seemed safe enough for the kids to play. The wind filled me with fierce and primitive joy, and I ran and ran and ran through fields of grass, leaping into the air, amazed when a gust would catch my skinny body and push it back so I landed in the same place I had launched from. I felt that the wind and I had become a single force, shaving the grass, whipping the lake into a foaming frenzy. I swallowed a bug—or, to be more precise, the wind blasted the unfortunate insect through my open mouth, and it slammed with sharp and startling force into the back of my throat. This did not disturb me at all. It added to my sense of glee. I was one with the wind, the grass, even the bug.

Not long after I told Angela the bedtime story about losing my teeth, I made contact with my old friend, who I hadn't seen in thirty years. As it turns out, we share a common interest in rock climbing. My friend's wife, a fine photographer and climber in her own right, has taken some great photos of her husband on various climbs. I learn that they are coming through Washington on a trip to Alaska. We arrange to spend a day at Index, a local granite crag. A few days before they arrive, I take another gander at some of the photos and remark to my wife that it looks like he has been leading some pretty hard climbs—a grade harder than anything I have so far led. "So?" my wife replies. (She has a knack for asking the right questions.) "I'm just saying," I mutter, with a hint of annoyance. Angela, peering up from her Calvin and Hobbes comic book, asks, "Is this the same guy you raced against in the fifth grade when you knocked out your teeth?" "Yes," I answer. She trades a certain look with her mother, and I feel compelled to add, "I'm not in the fifth grade anymore." My wife remains silent, just keeps cooking those eggs. Maddening, how she manages to say nothing and something at the same time.

It starts early, this need to compare one's self to others. I am most blessed when I can escape it. Perhaps one reason for this is that I'm not really very good at anything. I think another (and more interesting) reason is that a certain freedom, a lightness of being, comes from the dissolution of ego. As a kid, I was instinctively drawn to running and climbing. There are various reasons for this, but certainly one reason is that in these activities I felt free of the need to measure up to anyone's expectation. Although I was an active and fairly athletic kid, I was lacking in the self-confidence and aggressiveness that distinguishes a kid on the playground or in team sports. I was always afraid that under pressure I would mess up, and this anxiety led me to try too hard—which, paradoxically, dooms one to awkwardness when grace is most essential. I was the kid who ran all over the basketball court but never got the ball.

I loved to be alone in the woods, where no one was watching and I was free to be capable. I loved running along the pipeline road near my home, scrambling on the boulders of Mount Elden, climbing in the ponderosas as high as I could get. I found myself by losing myself in the immediacy of nature and the rhythms of my own exertion. This state of being is not characterized by reflective thought; on the contrary, it is characterized by the absence of reflective thought. There is, in moments of rapt attention, an evaporation of the self into an ocean of sensation during which the boundary that we usually feel between the physical and the spiritual melts away. This can't happen, for me at any rate, when I am keeping score.

Twenty years after I ate a bug in a windstorm, I was the third baseman on a church softball team in Missoula, Montana. I liked playing third base. I liked the line drives, the need for sudden bursts of speed. I discovered in myself the competitive spirit that I lacked as a child. Unfortunately, despite the presence of some good athletes and power hitters, our team had a miserable record. The reason—or at least the most evident of a few reasons—was our right fielder, Richard "Pot-Shot" Potter. Pot-Shot was a burly man, strong as a bear, with an arm like a cannon. He was also developmentally disabled and a resident of the men's group home my first wife and I managed together. Pot-Shot loved softball but didn't grasp the point of the game. He would lumber toward the ball (never did I see Rich run with urgency), pick it up slowly, and then fire it as high and as far as he could, vaguely toward whoever yelled at him the loudest. Many times in practice we patiently tried to coach Pot-Shot. He should throw the ball to someone in particular—anyone, really—and we would try to tag the runners "out" before they crossed home plate. "Do you understand, Rich?" He would nod and say "uh-huh."

And then, next game, he would trot out to scoop up right field grounders, wind up his cannon arm with every ounce of spirit he had, and hurl the softball into some distant pocket of sky as if he and God were playing a game of catch. Upon discovering this tendency, the members of an unscrupulous team (and there are some in church league) would shout just as loudly at Rich as we would, and likely as not the ball would come crashing down with stunning force on the opposing team's dugout just a couple of seconds after runners from each and every base rounded third, where I was helpless to hinder them. If the batters on the opposing team knew how to aim their hits toward right field, the innings were long indeed. Eventually, we'd manage three outs, and Rich would come loping up to our dugout with a huge grin on his face. This is one of my finest memories of Missoula: Mount Sentinel and Mount Jumbo in the background, bathed in the beer-colored light of a summer sunset, and Richard "Pot-Shot" Potter high-fiving his teammates as he entered the dugout, saying, "Hoooboy! Lots of balls!"

In 1981 I played trombone in the jazz ensemble at Anchorage Community College. It was in this group that I met Mike—a kid with flaming red hair, an adventurous spirit, a thirst for spiritual experiences, and a true gift for jazz trombone. I, on the other hand, loved jazz band the way Pot-Shot loved softball, which is to say I put my heart and soul into it, but I probably wasn't an asset to the ensemble. I sat second chair, but sometimes there is a lot of difference between first and second chair. My tone was asthmatic and pinched, whereas Mike's was bold, full, and golden—like a sunset. I often felt inadequate when I realized the gap between Mike's talents and mine, just as I felt inadequate ten years earlier when I couldn't run fast enough. However, I loved the music, and when it was my turn to take a solo, the feelings of inferiority and the need to compare myself to Mike evaporated in the sheer joy of improvisation. I don't know how it sounded to an audience, but it sounded good in my head. Mike, God bless him, was gracious enough never to disabuse me of that notion.

We became friends. Sometimes we'd head out to the sea stacks along Turnagain Arm, where we scrambled up the shattered rock and watched the bore tides come in while we drank Guinness, ate brown goat cheese, and talked about Buddhism and Christianity. We chased a moose (bad idea), panned for gold at his family's claim on the Kenai Peninsula, and listened to recordings of Louis Armstrong, Duke Ellington, and J. J. Johnson for hours.

While we hiked through the Alaska wilderness, I shared with him my love of the desert. In particular, I spoke of an unnamed spring in the Grand Canyon, nestled at the base of the Redwall Limestone below Horseshoe Mesa on the way to Sockdolager Rapids. Seen from above, it was a tiny, blessed burst of vegetation where the water emerged from the ground into a thin thread of vibrant green as it snaked its way down through jumbled vermilion rock to vanish as abruptly as it began. Water in the desert—all the more precious because of its fleeting presence. It was, I said, a sacred spot. I described the deep alcoves of limestone, how echoes came back in waves.

I moved back to Arizona and didn't hear from Mike for a couple of years. One March night, he called out of the blue and said he was in Utah and was on his way to Flagstaff. He had one goal: to play his trombone at that spring, if I would take him there. So on a cold, windy March day we headed for the canyon.

We trudged and slipped down muddy switchbacks with Mike's trombone until we found a place where the Redwall Limestone formed a vast horseshoe-shaped amphitheater. Mike began with scales and arpeggios, which vaulted from cliff to cliff until it seemed there was a chorus of hidden trombonists perched on ledges throughout the canyon. We took turns playing the horn. We played Brahms, hymns, jazz standards—alternating soaring golden tones with delightfully fat and brassy-edged low notes. The music swirled through alcoves and spilled over ridges until it seemed to come from the sky itself.

As we were hiking out of the canyon, we encountered a backpacker who laughed when he saw the trombone case. The celestial music, as he described it, had spooked him; he had wondered if it might be Judgment Day.

Since that time, the canyon has become more crowded, even in its wilder sections. I would hesitate to do what we did again. The opportunity for silence and solitude is one of the best gifts of nature, and perhaps our music had been a crude invasion of someone's peace. But I can't say I regret it.

It didn't matter that Mike was a better trombonist than me. What mattered was that our peculiar decision to lug a brass horn down to Horseshoe Mesa—something that probably could have earned us a ticket or at least a lecture from a ranger—unfolded into an extraordinary moment in which the creativity of human beings dovetailed exquisitely with the glory of nature. It is not hokey, I hope, to attach the word *praise* to what happened, and where praise is present, ego blows away in the wind.

And so my friend who I have not seen in thirty years arrives, and, yes, it turns out that he is a better climber than me, and he has more hair. In fact, he has dreads. We went to Index, where jagged peaks jut into the sky above a river called the Skykomish—an apt name for a mountain stream that throws itself against boulders and is filled with steelhead that throw themselves upstream with equal vigor. We chose a fine three-pitch route up the wall and, like the steelhead, fought against gravity. I groveled my way up, not in fine style and taking a few falls, while my friend led all three pitches, clean. But that is not the point.

The point is that late that night, when I closed my eyes and drifted into sleep, I relived just how it felt to get a finger lock in the thin crack of "Slow Children," to lay back against a sharp arête, step gingerly into a delicate stem, have my feet hold, and take just one second to look across the valley at the splendid north face of Mount Index and the quicksilver ribbon of Bridalveil Falls tumbling through the forest of Douglas fir, western hemlock, and Alaska cedar. I once again sensed the sun on the back of my neck, smelled the breeze infused with the resin of all those trees, and felt in my throbbing fingertips the texture of granite on crimpy ledges. And that is the same feeling, or pretty damn similar, to running into a hurricane wind, playing trombone in the Grand Canyon, or firing softballs as high and as hard as you can just for the sheer holy hell of it. So what if someone does it better? The point of the game is joy. Even a forty-seven-year-old man, ordinary in all respects, can feel it. And I can keep the rest of my teeth.

THREE ARIZONA CANYONS

I. LET'S BEGIN ON State Route 260 as it promises escape from the fast food joints and mobile homes of Camp Verde. Let's say you are driving through a thunderstorm—the first of the summer monsoons. The sky is charcoal blue with a gathering downpour, and the breeze feels electric, with a hint of ozone. In thirsty anticipation, the desert is opening up. The pungent aroma of the creosote bush prompts you to roll down the window, even though the wind buffets your face. The highway is empty and the landscape wide open as a heart. Shimmering curtains of rain weave against a backdrop of ragged lightning and the sudden rip of thunder. The curtains tease the yearning ground. Swirls of wind shave the hills.

As you gain elevation, you leave the creosote behind. Soon, you are winding your way through gently rolling grassland the color of wheat, tinged with a hint of Kelly green, sparsely dotted with gnarled juniper and piñon pine. Gradually, elevation increases and trees crowd closer together. Isolated ponderosa pines begin to appear, and soon predominate. Grasslands give way to genuine forest, open, with a carpet of brown needles. The sky darkens and rain begins to fall, fat drops dimpling the dusty shoulder of the highway. Say the forest beckons you off the highway and onto a dusty road. You don't know where you are going, but you will go there. For several miles, the ponderosa forest seems changeless: furrowed dark bark, green needles above, brown needles below. It smells good. Lightning strikes frighteningly close to your car. Miles pass. Because you did not know and you can't see far ahead, you aren't prepared for the end of the road. There is no warning that you are about to come to the edge of a deep gash in the landscape. It is, the map says, West Clear Creek. What the map can't show is the sound of wind and the feeling of smallness that can suddenly swallow a human being. *What's down there?*

West Clear Creek snakes its way through a splendid narrow canyon for thirty miles before widening out into a broad desert canyon in its lower ten. In its upper and middle course, West Clear Creek is lush, remote, difficult to travel through, and stunningly beautiful. Hikers who venture the full length of the canyon have to swim through pools where the canyon walls completely hem them in—similar to the more famous Narrows of Zion Canyon. The cream-colored and lovely Coconino sandstone, with its cross-bedding and blocky structure, is reflected off of clear, cold pools. Dense vegetation lines the banks.

There are several trails into West Clear Creek, but the most interesting descent is through one of the spectacular side canyons that come in from the south. These canyons start as shallow, modest draws in the pine forest, but then quite abruptly slice into the Coconino Sandstone, forming serpentine and foreboding slots with sudden dropoffs and deep "keeper" potholes. Such canyons—Bear, Sundance, and Wilbur, just to name three of the best—offer challenges to experienced canyoneers with climbing equipment. They may offer death by hypothermia or a broken neck to those not careful or prepared.

On a dry day I've come to Bear Canyon, the easiest of the three, with my daughter Jordan and her boyfriend, Austin. They are from Seattle, and I want to show them the country where I grew up. As we scramble down into the slot, the hot, dusty air of July is replaced by the cool dampness of a canyon that has year-round pools never warmed by daylight. A single shaft of sunlight slips through a keyhole gap and illuminates the ledge from which our first rappel takes us. Dust motes twirl lazily in the sunbeam. I set up the anchor and down we go.

A slot canyon is a world of curves. Rappelling into a slot, one sees neither the top of the canyon nor the bottom—only bowls, scoops, hollows, grooves, waves, ridges: an infinity of perfect curves, swirling in all directions at once. These curves bring joy to both the fingers and the eyes. In Bear Canyon, the creamy buff-colored Coconino Sandstone is cool, gritty, pleasing to touch. Nestled into small niches in the stone are delicate moss gardens, testament to the seeping moisture that finds its way from the porous soil above through jointing in the rock layer. In some places I can feel both walls at the same time, tracing each parallel ridge and groove carved into the stone by raging flash floods.

"The curve," my grandfather told me when I was about ten years old, "is the most perfect of God's ideas. That's why Woman is the jewel of creation. And Snake—a backward curve—is an abomination." Then he told me to go outside and play. And so, puzzling over his incomprehensible parable, I explored the woods behind his house, and I saw curves everywhere: the path of a heron's flight, a spider's web, a slithering snake. An infinity of curves, playing with each other, penetrating each other, intertwined. I wondered which of the curves were backward and therefore sinister, and which followed God's trajectory. How could I tell them apart? What was I supposed to see?

My grandfather was a large, deep-voiced man with a King James vocabulary and the bearing of an Old Testament prophet. I remember that he put applesauce on everything he ate, as if this too was part of God's ordained plan. Before meals, he offered endless, rambling prayers in which he managed to work in the most obscure stories from the Bible and thanked God for things such as the veins in a sassafras leaf. What did he mean with his story of the perfect curve? Maybe my grandfather meant that spirits inhabit everything. Maybe he meant that the world was both seductive and dangerous. Maybe he was just telling me to be careful. Then again, maybe it was just a joke. After all, the man put applesauce on his pork chops. Whatever his intent, the result was that I understood the physical and spiritual realms to be intertwined, in ways that could lead to pleasure or to trouble.

Every turn in a slot canyon leads to a surprise: perhaps a delightful fern garden, or a patch of poison ivy. Maybe a row of perfectly formed bathtub potholes, or a pocket of quicksand. Maybe the carcass of an elk that fell into a pool and couldn't get out . . . and you now have to swim through rotten elk stew. You are at the mercy of the curves; you go where they lead, be they forward or backward. Exploring a slot without a rope—or with a rope that is too short—is an exercise in anxiety or faith, however you choose to see it.

But today, there is no such anxiety. Bear Canyon is mild; only three short rappels. Still, the rappels are directly into deep pools, and there are freezing swims through inky black water. It is adventurous enough for today. After a while, the slot opens up, and it's boulder-hopping on water-polished stones to the confluence of West Clear Creek. Along the main creek, dappled light dances through maples and reeds. Puffy cumulus clouds skitter across the high country Arizona sky, so blue you could swim in it as well.

It must be that some of the curves of Bear Canyon are "backward," or we would simply have traveled in a circle. I can't help but think that all the curves of this day, both those of Woman and those of Snake, came together in perfect harmony and symmetry to shape this canyon that is the exact shape of my notion of paradise.

II. BEFORE I WAS old enough to seek out more remote and wild canyons, before I was old enough to disdain the claptrap of tourism, I loved Oak Creek and its canyon with the simple and boundless love of a child. On Sunday mornings I went to church and I believed what I was told there, but it didn't really interest the ten-year-old me. I preferred Sunday afternoons. As soon as the Sunday ritual of pot roast and a couple chapters of Scripture were dispensed with, it was time to call my friends, Paul and Danny, and see whose parents were willing to take us to the canyon for the church of Oak Creek and its different set of sacraments. We'd skitter from rock to rock with paper cups, catching crayfish, or scramble over blobs of Supai Sandstone, or muster the courage to jump off the cliffs at Grasshopper Point.

Sedona, before it had vortices, was a cheesy town inhabited by cranky John Birchers who painted lurid sunsets and shot rock salt out of pellet guns at skinny little kids like me who snuck into their orchards to eat green apples. No Pink Jeeps. No teal arches. No medicine wheels. My oldest sister got married at the Cowpies on Schnebly Hill Road. My brother played Vivaldi on his trumpet. It echoed off the cliffs. Now there are medicine wheels on the Cowpies. Under the influence of the vortex, people have visions there. Under the influence of various substances, people had visions there in high school, too.

After a few years, the sacraments evolved: rock climbing at the overlook, skinny-dipping in the moonlight, midnight hikes up West Fork with college girls and a six-pack of beer. Grasshopper Point was the place to go when we ditched school, on, say, the first freakishly warm day in March when the air hinted spring but the shock of the water plunged us back into scrotum-shriveling winter.

With various friends or on my own, I explored Pumphouse Wash, bushwhacked deep up West Fork's side gulches and promontories, hiked up Wilson Mountain, over Sterling Pass to Vultee Arch, scrambled in Secret Canyon or Boynton Canyon, and climbed out on the girders of Midgley Bridge as far as we dared. I remember midnight drives with my friend, Dave, in his Cadillac, with the Allman Brothers or Stephen Stills in the tape deck.

Some of the best nights were by myself, in winter, with a thermos of hot spiced tea. Maybe I'd hike up to the waterfall above Encinoso or up to Brins Mesa. Maybe I'd take the Schnebly Hill Road from the top and park at the basalt cliffs on the canyon's east rim. I'd take a walk through the crunchy snow, under a quicksilver moon, full of the juice of youth and a thirst for life.

Things change and don't change. When I come back to this canyon three decades later, I slip easily into a landscape that is as familiar to me as the floor plan of the house where I grew up. Driving up the winding (and to tourists, somewhat treacherous) highway, I need only lightly rest my forearm on the wheel; I know each curve before I even reach it. The exact shape of each rocky outcrop on the road's shoulder is imprinted in my memory. A deep joy settles into my bones at the sound of the creek as it burbles its way through the obstacle course of rounded gray basalt and rusty red sandstone boulders. When I stop at familiar creek crossings, my feet still know the pattern of hops necessary to get to the other side.

And yet, a profound sense of loss coexists with the joy. I will never live here again. If it were up to me, the thousands of people who now live within a few miles of the creek would go elsewhere. As more and more people have come here to celebrate the *spirit* of this remarkable place, more and more of that spirit—for me, at any rate—seeps away. The canyon is cluttered with bungalows. Sedona wallows in pretentiousness. Humans have been hard on this canyon.

Some of it is selfish; I simply liked it better the way it used to be. I liked hiking in West Fork when a narrow dirt path led past an old abandoned ranch house and its apple orchard. I remember sneaking my way through all the rooms and sheds, looking for the kind of treasures an eight-year-old boy loves: rusted old farm implements, meat grinders, drill bits, license plates. I liked Grasshopper before it had a fee station, back when a car full of teenagers could go there at night, build a campfire, go skinny-dipping, and not get ticketed.

But some of the sense of loss is more profound and not centered on my own nostalgia. The landscape itself has changed, in ways that are subtle and ways that are not. For instance, a part of the canyon that many consider the most scenic and enchanting—the western slope just south of Slide Rock, in the area around Sterling Pass—shows the ravages of fire. In this area, rusty rounded shelves of Supai Sandstone merge into abrupt cliffs of buff-colored Coconino Sandstone. Nestled into shady north-facing alcoves are verdant pocket groves of ponderosa, Douglas fir, and the peculiar bluish-green Arizona cypress. An implausibly blue sky completes the picture, in one of the most startling contrasts of color I have seen anywhere in nature. In October the bright crimson of vine maples makes it even better. Or at least, that's how it used to be.

The Brins fire of 2006 ripped up these slopes, leaving in its wake a forest of charred snags. While such an event, in and of itself, might be a natural occurrence and not a tragedy, those who call northern Arizona home know that the problem is not one particular fire. It is the cumulative effect of many fires—more than there used to be or should be. And the fires are getting bigger and burning hotter. While fire is an unavoidable and even desirable event in the semi-arid forests of northern Arizona, the fires of the past two decades have been devastating.

The causes are numerous and interwoven. A long history of questionable forest management practices has allowed the build-up of lower-story fuels on the forest floor. The number of dead and dying trees due to both beetle infestations and drought stress has increased. And finally—though some, including Arizona politicians, dispute the contention—climate change has made summer temperatures hotter, winter snowpack sparser, and the crucial monsoons more erratic. The worst of these fires have occurred not in the canyons but in the vast forests that cover the Mogollon Rim, above the canyons.

Like many of my friends and relatives, I remember when the Dude fire ran through the Mogollon Rim country near Payson in 1990. It burned twenty-eight thousand acres and was the largest wildfire in Arizona history at that time. We were impressed by the extent and the ferocity of the burn, but today, it doesn't even make it into the top five.

Arizona's worst wildfires have occurred in the past two decades, and the very worst have happened in the past decade. My hometown of Flagstaff, just twenty miles from Oak Creek, has seen its share of trouble, most recently with the Schultz fire of 2010. Viewing the impressive mountain panorama of the San Francisco Peaks and Mount Elden from the east—where I used to live—one now sees a wide-angled view of ashen wasteland. It used to be one of the most inspiring views in Arizona.

In 2002 the Rodeo-Chediski fire claimed more than 468,000 acres—and over 110,000 in a single day. And in 2011 the Wallow fire topped them all, burning an astounding 568,000 acres of forest in both Arizona and New Mexico. These fires burned so hot that they sterilized the ground itself, killing the many microorganisms that inhabit the top foot of soil. This in turn affects the watersheds of the many canyons that drain the Mogollon Rim, as the forest is both the source of and the filter for the creeks and springs that bring life to the desert below.

Whenever I return from a trip to the canyons of my youth, my heart is flooded by both contentment and sadness. Homesickness does not even begin to do justice to the complexity of the emotion. But for all the worry I have about the changes in the ecology, the primary feeling I carry with me is one of gratitude and peace. It is a great gift to have grown up in such a place, and a great pleasure to return to it.

Occasionally I will find myself in conversation with someone who mentions Oak Creek Canyon. Perhaps he went there for the first time on a recent trip. Or perhaps she took a Pink Jeep tour up to the vortex on Schnebly Hill Road and was overwhelmed by the sunset at the very cliff where the notes of a Vivaldi concerto once echoed at my sister's wedding. Or perhaps the traveler swam at Red Rock Crossing and then wandered up the creek to a trail that threads the needle between the towers of Cathedral Rock. More often than not, the earnest traveler will say something like *How lucky you are to have grown up there. It is such a spiritual place.*

I never quite know how to respond to a comment like that. Several possible remarks die on my lips: *We are very good at destroying spiritual places,* is one such remark. *Every place is a spiritual place,* is another. But usually I just smile and say, with a full heart, *Yes. Yes, it is.*

III. ANOTHER MEMORY FROM age ten: my older sister, Margie, taking me fossil hunting in Sycamore Canyon. It was like an Easter egg hunt. Margie was a geology major in college, and the stories she told me about the unfolding of the world were different from my grandfather's stories. "All of this land used to be under the ocean," she told me. And in my hand I held a piece of the ancient world. I remember how I felt contemplating those fossils: sort of overcome by the strangeness of everything. Is this common to ten-year-olds? I would turn the fossils over in my hand and say the names to myself: brachiopods, gastropods, cephalopods. They seemed so much more than calcified shellfish; they were mollusks in the image of God, rocks infused with spirit. I don't remember if I considered the stories offered by Genesis and paleontology incompatible. I don't know if I considered *why* and *how* two different questions.

Rugged Sycamore Canyon is sprawling and remote. It begins with deep-sliced basalt gorges near its headwaters. Below the basalt, Sycamore quickly cuts through Kaibab Limestone and Coconino Sandstone before broadening out in the Supai Sandstone Formation. Most of Sycamore is comprised of the Supai Formation, and, as is typical of canyons in this soft layer, the canyon loses its vertical walls. The rust-colored stone forms buttes and bluffs that are similar to those surrounding Sedona, farther to the east and in the Oak Creek watershed. One distinctive feature of Sycamore Canyon is that in its lower reaches it cuts through the much harder layer of Redwall Limestone, the same layer that forms the most dramatic and precipitous cliff band in the Grand Canyon. The vermillion, manganese-varnished Redwall holds many excellent fossil specimens.

Because of the complex interplay of elevation, geology, and climate, there is an astounding richness in terms of biodiversity, microclimates, and scenery. There is a profusion of niches. The canyon concentrates and conflates life zones that would normally be hundreds of miles apart had they been located on open ground. On north-facing slopes, deep clefts that rarely see sun hold snow patches well into late spring, while slopes at the same elevation on the opposite side are baking in the hot sun. At such an elevation and latitude, the sun's rays are intense. As a result, a protected pocket or small alcove among heat-holding rocks can have a warm microclimate even in January, when the forests are draped in snow. It is possible to have lush, wet pockets of typically alpine wildflowers just a stone's throw from Sonoran Desert vegetation like agave and mesquite. Deep pools of standing water in the bottom of narrow slot canyons remain frigid all year long.

As soon as one descends into Sycamore or one of its side canyons, the diversity and complexity of the ecosystem increases dramatically. Around every bend in the canyon, there is a different combination of slope, aspect, rock strata, soil drainage, and leeward or windward exposure. A protected south-facing pocket surrounded by black basalt boulders will bake like an oven and support only an ornery barrel cactus, while a north-facing alcove may stay cool and damp enough to support columbines and ferns. The variability of factors leads to many surprises, as plants can become established outside of their typical elevation zones.

I trace my lifelong love of topographic, climate, and geologic maps to my childhood desire to understand the canyon as a complex neighborhood, an unfolding narrative of alliances and histories. To my ten-year-old self, that narrative had the quality of part myth and part science.

Margie collected sand in mason jars, labeled them, and kept them in the garage. I played with the sand in those jars, pouring it out on a cutting board, making sand paintings, pouring it in again. I memorized words long before I knew what they meant: Cambrian, Jurassic, Mesozoic, sedimentary, igneous, metamorphic, overthrust belt, subduction zone, anticline, syncline, batholith, diatreme, Wingate, Kaibab, Dakota, Tapeats, Vishnu, diorite, dacite, andesite, rhyolite, basalt. I studied geologic maps that I didn't understand, maps that spoke with authority, like Genesis, about the nature of things and the unfolding of time. Cross-sections of canyons that showed layered strata laid to rest one upon the other, for eons, like a list of "begats." And I kept those fossils in a shoebox under my bed.

SACRED PLACES

————

I. IT MAY SEEM a strange way to begin an essay about sacred places, but let me say that in all my years I have never encountered so splendid a latrine as the one on the edge of the Sulphide Glacier, just over the rock pile from high camp on the way to the summit of Mount Shuksan, in the North Cascades of Washington State.

First of all, allow me to acknowledge the competition, for there are many inspiring latrines in the world. (I'm speaking, of course, of places designated for the purpose, rather than those chosen out of desperate necessity.) For instance, there is (or was) an outhouse, sans door, just a short stroll from the West Rim Trail in Zion National Park, where one may sit and contemplate the drastically blue high-desert sky while a red-tailed hawk wheels lazily overhead, above an expanse of cream and burnt-orange sandstone temples.

And then there is another doorless outhouse a stone's throw from a cabin I used to live in a few miles outside of Fairbanks, Alaska. It was best in winter, when its contents were frozen solid. Granted, it was hard to get out of bed when the temperature was thirty degrees below zero, but once committed to the Styrofoam seat, one was free to appreciate the crystals of frost that laced the bare limbs of birch and willow, twinkling in milky-blue moonlight. The view looked out on typical subarctic bog forest, where spindly snow-tufted black spruce leaned drunkenly in all directions, like trees in a Dr. Seuss story. Once in a while, an aurora weaved overhead, emerald curtains rippling, spears piercing the night, violet patches of excited, magnetized stratosphere skittering like skipped stones across the black pool of sky.

But the winner, hands-down, is the open-air latrine on the edge of Sulphide Glacier. Once, in early morning, I sat there and watched car-sized bergs of ice on the Crystal Glacier slide from their tenuous perch and trundle into the basin of Sulphide Lake, a thousand feet below. The sound of the ice giving way echoed like the report of a gunshot, then dissembled into a deep rumble, finally ending in a puff of spindrift that belied the tremendous power of an avalanche. I couldn't see all the way into the basin below, but I imagined carnage. On many occasions in the mountains I have seen the trunks of enormous fir trees splintered by the power of snow and ice as casually as the drinker of a martini might splinter a toothpick. It took a while for the crackling sounds to completely thin out to silence.

I was alone, as one usually prefers to be in such circumstances. I don't know if I said anything. (Maybe I said, "Holy shit!")

What consecrates a sacred place? What makes it holy? And why, you may wonder, do I start my essay with outhouses? Why do I blend the undignified with the sublime? My answer is that I don't blend them; they come to us already blended. The spirit and the body are inextricably bound to one another. Why wouldn't it be fitting for a latrine to occupy sacred space?

This is as good a place as any to confess that I haven't regularly attended church in about twenty years. I don't miss it very much. Still, I admit a fondness for the words *sacred* and *holy*. Of course, I use the words how I wish to use them. And how do I wish to use them? Well, in a sacred place I fully inhabit both my animal and my spiritual nature. These components are equal; the animal nature is no less dignified than the spiritual nature.

Of course, *spirit* is a slippery word. I won't even attempt a definition. The word hints at something transcendent. But what, exactly? I resist notions of heaven; my sacred places are earthbound. Still, *spirit* is a word that I find compelling and useful. Everything is always changing, moving. One of the precepts of Buddhism is impermanence, or transience. Spirit is moving. Perhaps what is sacred is the elusive transference of life in nature. A wave moves through water but is not itself the water.

And what is holy? Perhaps the most humble of things. The fertility of soil, for instance, depends on organic matter—or what we sometimes call *waste*. Worm castings. Rotting roots. Manure. A colony of oyster mushrooms feeds on a nurse log, and the tendrils of mycelium bring nutrients and water to the living plants that sprout from the corpse. Consider the complex chemical interactions between billions of microorganisms in every teaspoon of soil. Among those interactions, we understand the imperatives to survive and reproduce. We understand eating, mating, drinking, shitting, and so forth. But there is something, I think, that eludes our understanding. Religions try, with limited success, to get at it.

A sacred place, to me, is a place where I feel connected to other creatures, sustained by water and earth, and part of the intricate choreography of molecules that we call *nature*. It is a place where I feel—simultaneously—my insignificance in the universe, and my centrality in it. In a sacred moment, in a sacred place (and I find it hard to separate moments from places), everything is inexplicable in its purpose, irreducible in its parts, uncontainable in its power. At the same time, the sacredness is elusive; it is made manifest in things, but it is not contained in things. Rather, it moves through things. We *inter-are,* as Thích Nhất Hạnh puts it. None of the components contains the sacredness; the sum of the whole is greater than the parts. What is the sum? It remains beyond our grasp. We can't add that high.

In shamanistic traditions, animals often function as spirit guides. I like that. It is a theology that acknowledges the sacredness of animals, and of the body. What is more mysterious than matter animated by breath, will, and consciousness? What is more miraculous than stardust rearranging itself over and over again—now as a pterodactyl, now as a spoon worm, now as Leonardo da Vinci, now as a hammerhead shark, now as a seventh-grade girl, and now as a malamute who appears suddenly out of the woods?

II. HE WAS A dog of exceptional intelligence and responsiveness. He was the best companion I could have imagined. Why did he appear out of the woods, inexplicably, and why did he follow me for four days? I don't know. Perhaps this is a mystery that can be explained by neither science nor religion. Who can probe the heart of a dog? But the coincidence of this particular dog, in this particular place, on a fine summer week in 1982, is a good example of what, to me, is sacred.

The Kenai Peninsula, in Southcentral Alaska, is an excellent place to contemplate the braiding of the physical and spiritual worlds. In particular, the watershed of the Resurrection River as it tumbles northward from hills of wind-shaved tundra to the glassy fjord of Turnagain Arm is a glorious place. In its lower reaches, lush forests of spruce and hemlock alternate with swaths of dense willow and alder that outline the fan-shaped paths of avalanches. Bears often lurk in the thickets. Gradually, the valley bottom rises until, after a series of steps up heathery benches, one reaches the windy, cold, gravelly divide of Resurrection Pass.

I was only two miles into my four-day hike when I sensed that I was being followed. I turned around and there he was, staring at me with eyes the color of glacial ice. He was the archetypal malamute: keenly alert, erect of posture, deeper-chested than a husky, with a black-rimmed face. A stunning canine. He stood still, appraising me but without threat. It seemed he was waiting for me to decide something.

Surely he must belong to someone. "Go home!" I commanded. He looked back at me, calm as God, panting lightly. His answer, it seemed, was a good-natured no. So I began to hike again, thinking perhaps the dog would slink away into the woods from which he came. But he did not.

Once again, I admonished him to return to his home. Once again, the dog simply waited me out. We repeated this ritual several more times. Finally, I turned around and began hiking back the way I'd come, hoping I would encounter the dog's owners. He seemed content to follow me in either direction. I went a mile and met no one, heard no voices, saw no evidence of a campsite or cabin in the woods. Whenever I stopped, the malamute would stop too, and stare at me mildly. I called out "Hello! Hello! I have your dog!" but no one answered.

The day was slipping away and I had a long way to go. "Well, Dog," I said, "I guess you're my co-pilot." Since I didn't know his name and didn't expect to keep him, I simply called him Dog. He was a quiet companion; he didn't bark, whine, growl, or howl. He padded along softly behind me. Sometimes, when I didn't hear him for a long time, I thought he had finally given up the game and gone home, but then I'd turn around and see him trotting along, his placid, panting tongue framed by prodigious teeth.

Although he ignored my first command to go home, he responded immediately when I called him. He was clearly a well-trained animal. Whenever I stopped to rest, Dog would vanish for a time, then magically reappear precisely when I wanted to get moving again. My only worry—that he would run into a thicket, piss off a bear, and bring the bear back to me—proved unfounded.

He shared my food gladly but was circumspect in begging for it. At bedtime, he curled up near my sleeping bag and was in the same place in the morning. I have no idea if he roamed during the deep of the night.

It was a blessing to move with each passing day higher into the sublime landscape of tundra with a companion who did not feel the need of speech. The high point, both literally and figuratively, was the pass. I can close my eyes and see the wide sweep of heather-carpeted hills and the bleached white caribou skull that sat like a monument on the divide between watersheds. I smile at the memory of Dog sniffing at the bones then sitting next to me on his haunches as I surveyed the valley that we came from and the one we were going toward. It is the perfect picture of a sacred animal companion.

I didn't keep Dog. Everything moves, everything changes. In one of the most peculiarly perfect twists of the story, Dog did indeed find home again. More than a hundred miles away in Anchorage, I put posters on poles and bulletin boards, ads in papers. After a few days, I thought Dog was mine. In a final attempt to find his previous owners, I went to the dog pound—not to leave Dog there but to seek advice regarding what to do next and to check if anyone had been searching for a beautiful malamute. At the very moment I was leaving the pound to take Dog home for good, a bearded man ran out of his car, dropped to his knees, and exchanged lavish kisses with his missing malamute—who turned out to be not only a beloved animal but the bearded man's lead sled dog. It was clear that there was much affection between Dog and Bearded Man. It remains a mystery why, for one week, Dog blessed me with his allegiance.

That was more than thirty years ago. Dog is dead now; dead for a long time. But maybe not. Spirit moves through us all like a wave. If I were to go once again to Resurrection Pass, I would not be surprised to feel his presence, padding along a few feet behind me.

Nurse Log

———

PICTURE A BOY in the woods. He is ten years old. He carries a hatchet but is not using it. Instead, the boy aimlessly shambles around the corpse of a fallen Sitka spruce. He is a dreamy boy; if you spoke to him he might not hear you. It is not clear what he is doing. His dreaminess seems abnormal. Is it rapt attention? Autism? Idiocy? He is too young to be stoned. He just stares at the log. It seems he is talking to himself.

The rotting log is enormous—its girth greater than the boy's height tripled, and its length hard to discern in the dim light and dense undergrowth of the Olympic rain forest. The log is a world unto itself, intricate in its patterns of decay. Along the length of the log, a row of saplings has taken root: hemlocks, cedar, red huckleberries, and sprawling vine maples with roots splayed like a network of veins over the top and down the sides of the log. Shelves of fungi, like half-buried plates, nestle in the crotch where a branch as thick as the boy's waist meets the main trunk.

Because the boy is alone, he is free. Because he is free, his imagination is engaged. Too young to know what a fractal is, nonetheless the boy sees and instinctively understands that patterns repeat themselves at smaller and smaller scale: worlds within worlds within worlds. He sees, for instance, that a patch of moss in a shallow indentation is in fact a forest, and within that forest maybe there is a boy who sees a patch of moss, which is in fact a forest in which a boy sees a patch of moss . . .

He imagines that a tribe of ant-sized humans inhabits the log. Some of them live in the intricate labyrinth of ant holes bored into the rotten wood. Others live in the ferns and conks, which are, in fact, living buildings. The log is a world of neighborhoods linked by paths. A society lives on top of and within the log, a loose affiliation of tribal groups, each with its own customs, commerce, and systems of governance. There is an economy. There are bargains and transactions. Within the secret chambers of these plant homes, there are mechanisms and transformations that sustain the people. Years before the boy learns words like *xylem, phloem, cambium, stomata,* and *chlorophyll,* he imagines living buildings that breathe, that pump water, that turn light and soil into food.

There are three major pockets of growth on the log, where the wood has mostly turned to soil and the plants are thickest. These pockets, he decides, are the Upper Kingdom, the Middle Kingdom, and the Lower Kingdom. Each kingdom has its own art and music and mythologies, its own stories of heroism and love and war. He imagines secret wisdom and strange ceremonies under the canopy of ferns. Of course, there must be tests of endurance and skill by which boys become men and girls become women. And of course there are alliances and feuds.

There must be an illicit friendship between a girl of the Upper Kingdom and a boy from the Lower. They decide to meet on a secret ledge. So the boy makes a desperate climb from one part of the log to another in order to secretly visit the girl. The boy ascends a network of cracks and furrows on the tree's flank, nearly falling to his death a couple of times, until he arrives at a lush divot in the log, where there is a bed of moss and a pool of water in which he and the girl can swim.

Somewhere deep into his fantasy, the boy gets down very close to the log, gets on his belly, in fact, to look eye-to-eye at the startling, intricate, delicate face of decay. Gradually his stories about kingdoms and quests fade away as he notices the real creatures within the log: the banana slug, the crab spider, the industrious beetle. It dawns on him slowly that the log truly is a neighborhood, with its alliances and feuds and ambushes and heroic journeys undertaken because of love.

He is only a boy. He doesn't know that a nurse log holds, pound for pound, more life than any other same-sized patch of ground in the forest. He doesn't know that the white threads, thinner than hair, that he sees woven through the rotten wood are tendrils of mycelium spidering out from basal ganglia, and that the spongy mushrooms he sees are the fruit of a huge living net that knits the forest together. He doesn't know how the mycelium simultaneously feeds the new roots of living trees, and is fed, in turn, by the disintegration of the dead one. He doesn't know words like *symbiosis*. Neither does he know what has been planted in him, or what will grow from this. He knows only that the log is the coolest thing he has ever seen.

He is pulled out of his reverie by the voice of his father calling him. It is time for dinner. The boy runs back to the campfire where his parents and his older sisters await. His parents ask him what he has been doing. Embarrassed, he says he has been chopping wood with his hatchet. That is what a boy should be doing. Chopping wood. "Did you bring any wood back for the fire?" his father asks. The boy mumbles, "No, sorry, I forgot." He can't tell them he has spent an hour looking at a log, making up stories about the tiny people who live on it. He can't tell them that he shrunk, in his mind, to the size of a bug. That's a stupid thing to do. He's too old for that. It shall remain his secret.

Make a Joyful Noise

IN THE WINTER of 1994 I packed my belongings into a car that barely ran and moved to Seattle. I didn't know anyone there and didn't have a job waiting for me. The first work I found in the sloppy Seattle winter was digging the foundation of what was to become the Redhook Brewery. My second job was baking bread in a grim basement beneath the warehouse of a Chinese grocer in the International District. One day I returned to my car to find the windows broken, needles and pill bottles on the floor, and my sleeping bag unpacked and spread out in the back seat. I replaced the windows, and from that day on left the doors unlocked for whomever might seek refuge in my car. Soon after I quit, the bakery burned down under mysterious circumstances. After that, I took a succession of warehouse jobs in the poisonous industrial wasteland along the Duwamish River, loading things like ball bearings and frozen chickens onto railroad cars. My longest stint was at Romac Incorporated, a factory that made sewer pipe fittings.

I shared a house with two women, both painters, a block from Gasworks Park, where the intestinal pipes of an old refinery made a ghastly and beautiful silhouette against the waters of Lake Union and the skyline of downtown Seattle. It was a household of not much money but many hundreds of old and rare books, herbs in the garden, sculptures in the yard, and paintings in the studio. Courtney Love's astrologer lived across the street and was the first neighbor I met. Greeting me in her barren rose garden, she asked me how old I was. I told her I would turn thirty-three in about a week. "Thirty-three," she said ominously, "was not a good year for Jesus."

In an attempt to start my thirty-third year off on the right foot, I escaped the city and headed into the wilderness on my birthday. I went as far as my feeble car would take me then set out on foot in snow that was at first knee deep but soon became hip deep. I set my sights on a mountain in the Monte Cristo Peaks. Eight miles and four thousand feet later, I stood on its summit, exhausted, looking out at a sea of jagged peaks. I remember sinking to my knees and saying something like "God almighty." I didn't know the names of them, but I knew I wanted to climb every single one. It was the right way to start my thirty-third year. After that, I went to the mountains every weekend.

I had come to Seattle either somewhat lost, or somewhat free, depending on one's point of view. Previously, I had been living in Missoula, Montana, where my first daughter was born and my marriage had ended. The church I belonged to unraveled, and with it my net of certainties. Quite abruptly, in the middle of the decade during which a man is supposed to sink roots and make something of himself, I was adrift. After years of graduate school studying the triumvirate of poetry, philosophy, and theology, I was freezing my fingers hoisting frozen chicken carcasses onto railroad cars and killing my brain cells sniffing the toxic adhesives used to attach rubber mats to the inside of tapping sleeves. I didn't write much in those years, nor did I read. It seemed to me that both the Word of God and the words of humans had left me more confused than inspired, so I just tried to inhabit my body and keep things simple.

I didn't talk philosophy with my buddies at Romac. My spot on the assembly line was next to a gregarious fellow who moonlighted as a bouncer at a stripper bar. We became unlikely friends. We tried to outdo each other on the production line, to see who could crank out more tapping sleeves in an hour. He found it amusing that I could quote Bible verses at the drop of a hat. "In my life," he grandly boasted, "I have known over three hundred women—in the biblical sense!" He didn't understand why I spent weekends in the mountains instead of taking advantage of his generous offer to hook me up with three strippers at once. "They'll wear you out," he predicted. "You'll be walking like a duck for days."

I didn't take him up on the strippers. In those days, three things kept me sane and able to endure the mind-numbing monotony of building sewer pipes day after day. One was my daughter, Jordan. Another was my obsession with learning the landscape of the North Cascades. The third was my love of music, which I played at full volume, on my way to the peaks. I was filled with restless energy. In the next two years I would climb eighty mountains—a mark that fell short of my friend's feminine conquests, I admit, but then I suspect I spent more time with each mountain than he did with each woman.

All week long at Romac, I'd think only of the weekend. On my way home from work, as I planned the weekend climb, I would crank up Pearl Jam on the car stereo. Their album *Ten* was the soundtrack for my first year in Seattle, and my favorite song was "Release." A couple years later, *Yield* came out, and my new favorite song became "Given to Fly." It expressed the expansive feeling I got from a long, hard, solitary day in the Cascades. I didn't surf, but the song perfectly expressed the exhilaration I felt in the mountains, the sensation of being gathered up and lifted by a powerful force.

Plato said that music "gives soul to the universe, wings to the mind, and flight to the imagination," and Nietzsche wrote that "we listen to music with our muscles." There are certain songs that raise the hairs on the back of your neck, make you sit suddenly down, close your eyes, and catch your breath. There are songs that open up a hole in your heart, and you fall into it. There are songs that pick you up like a wave and carry you. Maybe they carry you back to the eighth grade, to your honeymoon, to a mountain summit, or to a quiet moment when nothing happened except that the world opened up and let you in. Maybe they carry you back into the presence of someone who has died. Maybe they plunge you into an ocean of longing or grief or joy, and suddenly you are treading water where there is no bottom and no shore. There are songs that obliterate time.

"Given to Fly" captures, for me, the joy of inhabiting a body. The surfer is a conduit for the power of nature, an extension of the wave itself. I hold this connection to nature sacred. All of my climbs are indelibly etched in memory. I can close my eyes and picture the lay of the land from each summit. These moments are personal encounters with the landscape, and I cherish them with the tender affection that I used to hold for doctrines. I'm not about to claim that I know what these experiences mean. This feeling of connection—to a wave, to a mountain—isn't religious in any conventional sense. I'm less concerned than I used to be with the meaning of life and more concerned now with the celebration of it. It seems to me that the physical and spiritual selves are held together in a tight weave, and as I get older, music and sports have become the primary avenues through which the life of the spirit infuses and inspires the body.

It has become harder in recent years to get to the mountains as often as I used to, and so I've shifted some of that restlessness that fueled climbing into a new sport, track and field, which requires less planning and travel time. "Given to Fly" is still the one song I always listen to before a race. I listened to it before running the 200 at a meet in Colorado. The song, as it gathers itself like a wave and explodes, reminds me to explode out of the blocks and then run relaxed—like flying. It is difficult to explode and relax at the same time; it seems to be one of those pesky paradoxes that always lurk in the dark center of life—like the odd marriage of compassion and non-attachment, or finding your life by losing it. I can't think too much about how it happens; I trust the song to help me feel it.

At the Colorado Invitational, trying to calm my pre-race jitters, I lay down in the grass and listened to my song. I pictured surfers riding through perfect tubes of turquoise water, but the surfers I imagined ended up getting crunched and rolled by the unconcerned waves. I tried, then, to visualize my own upcoming race, and instead my mind zipped back to a meet about two months ago, on my forty-eighth birthday. On that occasion I wasn't particularly relaxed as I strained to eke out a victory against a competitor and did a face-plant across the finish line. As the spirit strained, the body failed; too much lactic acid. I am becoming well acquainted with such experiences as I train for the most brutal of races, the 400-meter dash. In no other event is the cruel disconnect between the spirit's desire and the body's limitation so evident. Perhaps I have a perverse Calvinist fascination with the 400 meters. It reminds me of a childhood game called Who Dies the Best.

Like most great games, the premise of Who Dies the Best was simple, but the execution allowed for creativity, daring, and subtlety. It worked like this: A kid would run across the lawn as fast as he could, while another kid pretended to kill him with some sort of projectile weapon. The method of assassination would vary: hand grenade, tomahawk, poison dart, machine gun. Sometimes we'd get more creative and come up with ingenious booby traps, trip wires, vampire bats, or bee swarms—anything that might bring down a moving target. Whatever the weapon of choice, the runner's job was simply to die and make it look good. It was the coolest game ever.

The neighborhood boys, like a panel of judges at the "Olympics of Death," debated the merits of each performance. Because the victim was running full speed, an essential part of the spectacle was, of course, the wipeout, which involved a good deal of flailing and tumbling. Extra points were awarded for a complete disregard for personal injury. Artistic interpretation also mattered. We paid attention to every groan, every shudder, every last twitching finger.

One of the keys to a good high-speed wipeout was to go limp at the correct moment and let the body follow its own logic as it crumpled to the cold, indifferent earth. You couldn't plan how to go down. Dying people, as everyone knows, don't protect themselves from an awkward fall. If you tried to plan it, it never turned out as cool as you imagined it would. You could control your trajectory, your speed, and your inner motivation, but the way in which your body collapsed had to be exquisitely random. This was not Aikido; it was death. Over-the-top histrionics backfired if they looked fake. It took an artist to make it realistic, effortless, and spectacular all at the same time. And the game was subject to a paradox that follows us all through life: it's possible to try too hard. As with almost any sport or art, to "die the best" required a combination of total commitment and complete relaxation.

It didn't seem to bother anyone what we were doing. We were boys. Parents didn't pay much attention to what went on outside anyway. If my memories of the game are fond, it is because it had nothing to do with real death. It was, in a peculiar boyhood way, a celebration of life. After all, no one stayed down. A kid could get up off the ground, laugh, and do it again.

There have been times in my life when music and movement have kept me feeling alive when I might otherwise have gone numb or crazy. In the spring of 2006, I slipped into a deep and isolating depression. I thought that I had irrevocably damaged my relationships to those who matter most to me, and no amount of talk could lift my spirit. But I was lucky enough at that time to have a job as a route-setter at a small rock climbing gym where I often worked alone and had complete control over the CD player.

I set routes as I listened to my favorite songs. Losing myself in music and movement was the best possible medicine. I named routes after songs: "Ball and Chain," "Fat Man in the Bathtub," "Walk the Line." The songs and the routes became linked in my mind, as if each song were suggesting a sequence of moves. Routes, like songs, had distinctive moods—some aggressive, some reflective, some quietly tense, some compressed and tight, others expansive and legato. Some routes were joyful, even in the midst of my depression. Musical phrasing suggested kinetic phrasing; each song unlocked a sequence of moves, from balance to imbalance and back again.

I named one route "Internal Light," after a song by the Seattle soul band Maktub. It was the best route I ever set. Not the hardest, but the best. Somehow, the spirit of the song fit the character of the moves. Like Janis Joplin's rendition of "Ball and Chain" or Johnny Cash's cover of "Hurt," Maktub's brilliant song is one that simultaneously hurts and heals when I listen to it. It reminds me that I must dive headfirst into the ache of my life if I hope to understand anything at all. It is a song filled with intertwined spiritual and physical hungers. It awakens in me a desire to connect with another person, and yet makes me aware of my essential isolation. It's a song about being and not being satisfied at the same time.

The lyrics of "Internal Light" demanded that I set a route full of quiet static tension, a long and sustained traverse characterized by deep stretches and delicate shifts of balance on small edges. It started with thin hands in a crack, shifted to a layback, then a series of crimpy side-pulls around a corner and some tricky stemming. A contemplative route with no big moves. The challenge was to stay on the wall and breathe. Although I didn't think of it at the time, perhaps I was illustrating the tension of love pulling one way and loss pulling the other. After I set the route, I remember sitting in the gravel with my eyes closed as the song built up to its crescendo, letting it wash over me like a wave: *I'm alive, alive, alive, alive, alive . . .*

In real life, it's hard to say who dies the best, and it is a pointless question. After all, it's not a competition. Dying is a solitary journey so personal, so inscrutable that our attempts to characterize it seem to be more about the living who are left behind—about our need to comprehend what is beyond comprehension—than they are about the dying. We may say of someone that he or she died peacefully or fearfully or fighting or without regret. These are the interpretations that we, the living, impute on the dead. Who is to say what it is like? The person dying is already in a country we can't visit. Religion has its own irrefutable answers, which some of us accept, some of us reject, and some of us hold up like a white elephant gift at Christmas, uncertain of their utility.

It is April as I write this. It's the season of new growth, new life. It's the season of boys playing games in the grass. It's the season for track meets, and it's the season to start getting up into the high country. It is also, paradoxically, a season of death and decline. I had breakfast today with a good friend, a widow who lost her husband exactly a year ago. Her husband was a well-known Seattle climber who was my friend and, briefly, my employer. My job was to construct a path and railing along a steep hillside so he could enjoy the wooded bluff on which he lived.

At first, I thought he would resent the railings. After all, he was a legendary mountaineer who was known to run up forty-four flights of stairs in the Columbia Tower with a backpack full of law books, who summited Denali at age sixty-four, and who climbed the famous Joshua Tree route, Illusion Dweller, at age eighty-three. But it was soon evident that even the bluff behind his house was now a mountain beyond his means.

Some days I didn't work on the path at all. Instead, I would sit with him and drink tea and eat donuts as we gazed out at the slate gray sheet of Puget Sound, pierced here and there with rays of elusive late winter sun. Sometimes he would want to speak, and sometimes he would want to just sit and contemplate Mount Constance across the water. It became clear that companionship was part of the job—perhaps the more important part. The gathering fog of Alzheimer's had not yet diminished his dignity, his gentle humor, or his gracious attentiveness. We spoke of many things, but most often we spoke of mountains. He was delighted to discover that we shared some favorite Cascade sanctuaries. He held the memories of many summits in his head, and he visited them like old friends— but I could tell that he was disturbed by how fuzzy the once precise memories had become. I wondered if the memories, in their singularity, would eventually wink out one by one to be replaced by a dreadful blankness, or if they would melt together into one archetypal memory into which he could slip, like a daydream.

The path was perhaps a quarter mile, through a magnificent wood of madrona and bigleaf maple, above the sound of constant, gentle surf. I cleared the slope of blackberry thickets, chainsawed my way through tangles of landslide debris, buried massive logs to stabilize erosion-prone sections of trail, and pounded hundreds of bamboo culms six feet into the ground. But before I could finish the project, my friend died. In the end, most of the railings were for naught; he couldn't walk the path beyond the first pair of chairs set to view the sunset over Mount Washington, across Puget Sound. He has no need of railings wherever he is now. A self-described "Bertrand Russell rationalist," he may not have expected an after-life; as an agnostic, I cannot say if he found one. But I like to think that after he quietly stopped breathing, as he was looking across the water at the Olympics, he just kept climbing higher into the alpine.

Actual death, particularly the incremental death of Alzheimer's, is different from the glorious gymnastics of our childhood game. It causes young boys to not want to visit nursing homes. The move-ments of the dying are often small—fingers curled tight around a bed rail, the ceaseless working of a jaw that has no food to chew, or a frail hand grasping for objects that are not there. These small movements can go on for a long time, longer than a boy would find it in himself to watch. Small as the movements are, it is clear that they come from a distress that is far bigger on the inside than it is on the outside. There is a book by Patti Davis about Alzheimer's called *The Long Goodbye*, and it is an apt title.

Just a couple of weeks after my friend's death, my father-in-law, Barney Banton, died of the same disease. Barney was, as they say, "a scrapper." He did not go gentle into that good night. One of my en-during memories of him is how he would stay up all night—several nights—and walk around the hospital over and over and over again with his shuffling determined steps. He drove the night nurse crazy. He was supposed to stay in his room, but no one could keep him down. Delusional, sick with MRSA and a urinary tract infection, he resisted sedatives powerful enough to knock out a racehorse. He punched a couple of people—including me—who tried to keep him from pulling out his catheter. And he walked. He summoned a surprising amount of strength for an old man who seemed on the verge of death, and he walked all night long. He was going to walk his way to something that felt like resolution, and no one was going to stop him.

And he spoke, but not really to anybody. In his jittery rambling, he blurted snippets of tales from his boyhood or the navy, random phrases and supplications: something about Jim, and a man overboard, and his old man who was a traveling salesman and a bastard. We heard Masonic rites and the Lord's Prayer and startling obscenities. Sometimes he spoke in Japanese, but only to the Japanese nurse. What linked together the scraps of his thought? I don't know, but I think that he, like all of us, needed to locate himself in a narrative that involved connections and reciprocal relationships with other human beings. The cruelest part of Alzheimer's was that he felt that connection slipping away, and he no longer could follow the narrative. One day, he looked me in the eye and said, "I want to be a human being."

He was a human being—and a good one. Among Barney's most enduring characteristics were his devotion to his family and his persistent concern that he "do the right thing." He needed to know that he had fulfilled his duty. As chief petty officer, as a mason, Barney's life took its shape from ritual and ceremony, from being a member "in good standing." As the fog clouded his mind, it became hard for him to know if he was still in good standing. Anxiety became the dominant theme in his life. What was his duty, and how was he supposed to fulfill it? We tried to let him know that he had already done it. It was okay to rest.

On our refrigerator, we have a photograph of Barney in an earlier time, as we would like to remember him. He's sitting in a chair at a beach, smoking a cigarette, looking at the camera with mischief in his eye and a characteristic half-smile. He's full of good-natured swagger. He looks like a guy who just pulled a practical joke on you, only you don't yet know it. I don't know for sure, but I'm guessing the photo is from the late fifties or early sixties. In another picture from the same time period, he is running with a wheelbarrow and in the wheelbarrow is a freckle-faced girl—my wife, Leann. He looks like a man devoted to his kids. He looks like a guy who knows how to jitterbug with his wife.

It's hard to say what Barney was aware of on the day he died. He had not been able to speak for quite some time, and I don't suppose anyone knows what was going on in his mind. Leann was holding his hand. We didn't know if he could hear much, but my daughter, Jordan, had chosen some music to play from her iPod. Sinatra seemed right for some reason, and when Ol' Blue Eyes began to croon the opening bars of "Come Fly with Me," something subtle changed in Barney, something ever so slight in the pressure of his grip or the ragged catching of his breath. There was a quickening in him, as if he were gathering himself up to go somewhere. It seemed the song was an invitation. Jordan went to find the nurse, to say that it was happening. Leann squeezed his hand and told him to go find Lee, his wife. "Go ahead, go dance with her." And then he was gone.

Some songs make you sit down suddenly, close your eyes, and catch your breath. What was once just a schmoozy nightclub tune to me will now be one of those songs. It has become a song that picks me up like a wave and carries me. It carries me back to a boat on Rosario Strait, where we scattered Barney's and Lee's ashes. Slivers of sunlight shimmied on the blue-green water as we watched the ashes mingle and dissolve. We tossed roses and drank a toast. And it carries me back further, to Barney's funeral, where, after the navy had its say, and the masons had their say, and the preacher had his say, my wife gave the shortest speech and spoke the truest and simplest words about a man to whom she had said the long good-bye. She ended it with music. And through joyous tears, she called my daughter out to dance with her. It was unexpected for such a formal ceremony, and it seemed for a moment that no one else quite knew what to do. Then I went out, with our other daughter. And then, one by one, in hesitant grace, aging and corpulent couples joined us, and the mason's hall became a dance floor. Some of those old people still know how to cut a rug. I could have sworn I heard the angels cheer.

I don't know what happens when people die, and I don't really know if Barney and Lee are doing the jitterbug up in the clouds somewhere. I hope so. The truth is, I don't think much about any world after this one, and I celebrate my father-in-law for who he was in this life. As a grower of plants and one who thinks often about nutrient cycling, I like to think that the dead are never really dead, but live on in the soil—or, in Barney's case, the water. In nature, the dead are constantly raised—not to the sound of trumpets, but rather to the slow drip of rain. It is not disrespectful to think that Barney's ashes might be fish food. The molecules of my body, too, shall someday dissolve and transform and become the daffodil that makes someone happy on the first warm day in March. As for that elusive thing called The Spirit—well, who knows? I have watched a few people die, some of them believers in an afterlife, some of them not. In every case, I have sensed something ineffable, something utterly beyond my grasp. I don't suppose that either a scientist or a preacher could explain it to my satisfaction.

Human ashes are a strange substance. Gray, gritty, not unlike volcanic ash. What is a human life worth, anyway? About ten dollars in chemicals is one answer; the sum of all existence is another. The mystery is that we exist at all, and that we can love. The marvelous thing is that we can have reciprocal, generous relationships with one another and with the whole living, splendid world. In studying the chemical processes that occur at the cellular level in plants, I have been struck not by how different plants are from animals but by how similar. All life is connected. What is a seed worth? I keep trying to persuade my daughter that the single most miraculous thing in the world is a simple seed. It is far more impressive than an iPad or a bullet train or the Taj Mahal. The nun Julian of Norwich had a vision in which the Lord appeared to her with a small nut in His hand. "It is all that has been made," He told her.

I don't know why spring has become the season of death by Alzheimer's. I sure didn't ask for it. Last week I went to Colorado to visit my aging father, who is starting to not recognize the woman he has slept next to for sixty years. He is not yet at death's door, but he is declining, both physically and mentally. I was talking to my mother about how hard it must be to have him fail to recognize her, and it came to us that a man with dementia is like an onion:

layers peel away, you say good-bye to them, and then there is a new layer. Just as the onion is the same onion without its outer layers, the man you are with is the same man, yet parts of his identity fall away. What is at the center of him?

Reading an essay called "Music and Identity" by the neurologist Oliver Sacks, I came across this passage:

> Music is part of being human, and there is no human culture in which it is not highly developed and esteemed. Its very ubiquity may cause it to be trivialized in daily life: we switch on a radio, switch it off, hum a tune, tap our feet, find the words of an old song going through our minds, and think nothing of it. But to those who are lost in dementia, the situation is different. Music is no luxury to them, but a necessity, and can have a power beyond anything else to restore them to themselves, and to others, at least for a while.

The last time I visited was in December, just before Christmas. The best memory of that trip involves music, which may not be at the very center of my father's identity, but it is pretty damn close to it. And as Pearl Jam is to me, as Sinatra is to my father-in-law, so Handel is to my father. Handel's *Messiah* is perhaps his favorite piece of music, and so it was an essential part of the Christmas season that we find a sing-a-long. We found one, at a sprawling mega-church on the outskirts of town, and on a blizzardy December night, we went.

The dismal, institutional cheeriness of the church gave me the willies, and I could imagine no circumstance other than the one I was in that would lead me to darken the door of such a place. But I was there for my father. I didn't listen to the smarmy pastor and his canned answers to my longings. His sales job was of no consequence to me. I was waiting, instead, for the music of George Frideric Handel to enter into the soul and body of my father and transform him from a tired, confused old man into the choirmaster that he used to be. It was a sing-a-long, by God, and we had come to sing.

My dad was nervous. He was afraid he would not remember the words or be able to follow the score. He didn't know if the bass

part—something he has always known like the back of his hand—
would come to him anymore. For days leading up to the event, I
had seen both worry and anticipation building up in my dad. The
day of the sing-a-long loomed like the day of an important test or
interview. He wanted to know, in his singing as well as in all other
ways, if he was the same man he used to be. Or, perhaps, he didn't
want to know. Each practice session we had increased rather than
allayed his anxiety, until, finally, I asked him if he, a choirmaster
for years and years, had ever kicked anyone out of a sing-a-long for
not knowing their part. That elicited a smile from him, at least.

We headed for the pews assigned to the basses and snuck into
the back, like bad boys in school. This was our refuge, here we would
hide out. But it turned out to be a miscalculation, for in the back,
there were no strong bass voices to help us along and cover up our
mistakes. Rather, we were surrounded by people who came not to
sing but to listen: mothers nursing infants, families with toddlers.
Not a deep-voiced man in sight. My father and I were a misfit section unto ourselves: A good singer with Alzheimer's, and a bad singer without. Nevertheless, as the familiar strains of the opening over-
ture carried him along, I saw the worry lines on my dad's face relax.
The first words of the aria seemed directed, in particular, at him:

> Comfort ye,
> comfort ye my people,
> saith your God.

Gradually, as the night progressed, I saw a transformation in him.
He pulled off the trick that is essential to all sport, all art, all true
religion: the simultaneous presence of complete intensity and
complete relaxation. He didn't sing as well as he used to, of course,
but he sang with joy. He didn't really read the music, but he sang
surprisingly well—better than I did, in places—as the bass part
seemed imprinted onto his neural pathways, his sense memory, as
automatically as an expert kayaker executes the Eskimo roll without having to think about how he is doing it. He knew in his bones
how all these chords resolved.

I'm not sure which part of the *Messiah* is my father's favorite. I know he holds special affection for the "Amen Chorus," the "Hallelujah Chorus," and "The Trumpet Shall Sound." On that night, it was the latter piece that brought chills to the back of my neck—not because it was performed with any particular brilliance, but rather because I paid attention to my father's face as he listened to the words from Paul's letter to the Corinthians:

> Behold, I tell you a mystery,
> we shall not all sleep,
> but we shall all be changed
> in a moment, in the twinkling of an eye,
> at the last trumpet.

I don't know how to describe it adequately, but as the exultant trumpet line filled the room, it filled my father as well. As I watched his trembling hands, I understood that there was an expansive soul in a decaying body, and that the soul was reaching for something beyond itself.

> The trumpet shall sound
> and the dead shall be raised
> incorruptible.

My father's life has been built on what many would consider the mutually exclusive pillars of faith and reason. His reason is eroding, and I can only hope that his faith endures. For my own part, I wish neither to attack nor defend religion. I'm just not interested. I am an agnostic to the core, thoroughly unwilling to be certain about the existence of God or an afterlife. I'm less interested, anyway, in my father's God than I am in my father. What matters to me in Handel's aria is not the theology but the longing for life implicit in the soaring trumpet line. What interests me is the trajectory of the spirit. And I know that this aria has now slipped into the pantheon of songs that can take me out of time. I will never hear it again without seeing my father's hands and his face as they were on that night. It was an honor to sing alongside the choirmaster.

And it's a good thing that my dad and I were able to sing together last December, because he wouldn't be able to do it now. Time keeps moving, and it only moves in one direction. This past week with him has been both a blessing and a sadness. Much has been lost, but I am amazed, still, at the power of music in my dad's life. A few nights ago, he came into the room where I was reading and announced that he was going to bed. I said goodnight, and he went to his room, but a little while later he was up again. He wandered around aimlessly as if he was looking for something that was lost but couldn't remember what it was. He stood for a long while in the kitchen, opened the refrigerator, shut it, opened it again, shut it again. He picked up some envelopes and some keys, studied them without comprehension, and put them down again. Finally, he came and stood near my chair.

"Decided to stay up?" I asked. Poor word choice on my part, as his expression told me that decisiveness had nothing to do with it. "Why don't you lie on the couch, and I'll play some music?" I suggested. He lay down, and I put on a CD of hymns and began to sing along with it. He was almost instantly asleep. I kept singing. I knew them all by heart, and I haven't been to church in fifteen years. To my father, steeped in this music for many more years than I've been alive, these hymns are embedded deeper than propositional speech, deeper than mathematical proofs, deeper than any understanding of his identity that could be put on a résumé.

There are few things as beautiful and as vulnerable as a human body at sleep. Parents of young children know this, as they look upon a boy or girl who has finally, after a dozen books, drinks of water, and questions, gone to sleep. I have watched my daughters sleeping and wondered what was going on behind the delicate fluttering of their eyelids as they dreamed. But it is a strange thing to see my father this way, curled up on the couch like a child. How many times has he watched me sleeping? The next hymn began to play, and I recognized it as one of my father's favorites, "When

Peace Like a River." Many years ago, my father and I sang this song together at the funeral of a friend of mine.

> When peace like a river attendeth my way,
> when sorrows like sea billows roll;
> whatever my lot, Thou hast taught me to say
> it is well, it is well with my soul.

My father's right arm was partially pinned beneath him, but his wrist and hand were free and dangled slightly over the pillow. A small hand movement caught my eye. Was it just a sleep twitch? I kept singing the chorus, with its layered echo in the bass part:

> It is well, it is well
> with my soul, with my soul,
> it is well, it is well, with my soul.

The hand movement was not a twitch. It was unmistakable. In his sleep, in that country behind his eyelids where he is still a human being, my father, the choirmaster, was conducting.

All week long, a different song had been stuck in my head. It was a song called "Do Not Weep" by the Faroese folk singer Eivør Pálsdóttir. It is a typically Nordic song, with a sparse and sad and lovely melody. I don't know exactly why, but it had become the song that carried me through the week. I hadn't shared the song with my parents, and I didn't sing it out loud. Rather, I hummed it to myself, usually unconsciously.

Unless it is Johnny Cash or Patsy Cline, I don't typically share my music with my parents. They would not be able to withstand even ten seconds of Pearl Jam. My mother is hard of hearing, and my father likes things that are familiar. But on the last day of my visit, my father heard me humming as I got out of the shower. He wanted to know what I was humming. He said to me, "You are always humming that song." I asked him if he would like to hear it, and I put the earbuds in his ear and found it on my iPod.

My father was perplexed by the earbuds; he thought I was putting a hearing aid in his ear, the kind my mother has. When the music seemed to come from inside his head, he seemed even more surprised. His face furrowed itself into a countenance that could either be the face of deep concern or deep engagement. He listened intently to the whole song, and then he asked me to say the lyrics. I shared the first verse:

> Do not weep about the night
> though your wings are broken
> and do not weep about the dark
> though your songs are unspoken
> do not weep about the sun
> though it blinded your weary eyes
> 'cause it showed you to a different path
> with beams from paradise

Then he wanted to know who the singer was and where she was from. I tried to explain that she was from the Faroes, a cluster of windswept islands in the North Atlantic between Norway and Iceland. It proved too confusing. (When I said *Faroes,* my father heard *Pharaohs,* and imagined islands near Egypt.) Finally, I told him that she was from an island near Iceland, which was as close as we were going to get to the truth. I said that the music was like the landscape of Iceland—wide open and beautiful, uncluttered. I was surprised and delighted to see an old spark rekindle suddenly in my father, the lover of maps, and he insisted we get out a world atlas and find Iceland. He wanted to know all about the volcanoes and glaciers. He wanted to see pictures. And then he wanted to hear the song again. After it played, I recited the last two verses:

> Oh do not weep, my beautiful,
> your candle is still burning
> and I will make my loyal horse

take your heavy burden
so do not weep, my beautiful,
'cause darkness is but fleeting
and you'll wake up to a sunlit day
where sunlight is ever greeting

Each hum, each breath, each heartfelt sigh
can soothe your melancholy
and deep inside I do believe
you'll find a peace so holy
so do not weep my beautiful
'cause darkness is but fleeting
and you'll wake up to a sunlit day
where sunlight is ever greeting

As he was listening, I considered why the song might have put itself so insistently into my brain all week long. It did not escape me that my father's illness is like a darkness, and that he would like to wake up to a sunlit day. This time after the song ended he sat in silence a while before he spoke. "I don't know what it means," he said finally, "but I think she is saying good-bye to someone she loves."

This was not the last good-bye to my father; it was good-bye to only one layer of the onion. The next time I visit, he will be the same, yet different. And then one day he will be gone. Until that time, I will engage the man that is there. I will try to connect with him by telling a joke, looking at a map—and singing a song.

On my flight back to Seattle, the weather was perfect. I stayed glued to the window, listening to music as I read the landscape. I listened to my favorite songs, including "Do Not Weep," "Given to Fly," "Come Fly with Me," and "Internal Light." Then I turned off my iPod to sit in silence for a while. Soon, I found myself humming the "Amen Chorus." Twenty thousand feet below me, the mountains of Idaho were sharp, angular, structurally complex—each one different, yet also part of a pattern. I did not feel sad. Certainly, there are moments when I do, but looking out at the glorious Lost

River Range, I felt awash in the spectacular beauty of life. Transience is part of that beauty. I am lucky to be connected.

The "Amen Chorus" is my favorite part of Handel's *Messiah*. I like it in part because the lyrics are simple: one word, Amen, repeated over and over. Amen means "so be it," or "so shall it be." It has the power of the more famous "Hallelujah Chorus" but is less strident, less theological, and more expansive.

I have known plenty of agnostics and atheists who understand praise, and feel it in their bones. And I have certainly known believers from traditions other than Christianity who understand praise as well. In my opinion, the simplicity and generosity of the "Amen Chorus" invites all who hear it to acknowledge the mystery and glory and transience of the world. It invites us to celebrate. It is, for me, an affirmation of what is, a single word of praise directed at whatever it is that we hold sacred. For some, that praise is directed at God. It may also be directed at those we love. Once, on a hike, I found myself singing the "Amen Chorus," and felt that I was singing to the tiny blossoming phlox at my feet, the lichen-patterned granite, and the glacial tarn that took the burnished gold of sunrise and gave it back to the sky. As I hiked past every soon-to-die flower, every rock being slowly weathered by water, wind, and lichen, I felt "So shall it be. This, and whatever happens next."

As a student of ecology, I like to think that all of the people that I have loved and who have died are in fact still alive, but in a different form. That dodges the question of self-awareness, of course. After I die, will there exist—anywhere or in any fashion—a distinct consciousness that is recognizably me? I don't know. Maybe when my story is over, it is simply over. But what does *over* mean? Ecclesiastes says that there is nothing new under the sun, which is another way of saying that everything old is still with us. The first law of thermodynamics says pretty much the same thing. As Janis Joplin discovered on the train, "It's all the same fucking day, man."

Who is to say what death is like? Is it like being caught up in the clouds to the sound of a trumpet? Riding the biggest wave? Melting into nonbeing? Or melting into everything else? When it happens to me, will I have an awareness that the stuff of my body will soon dissemble to soil, and then be transported along the tendrils of mycelium to feed the trees? Where does the spirit go? Does it meet a Creator? It is hard for me to imagine disembodied spirit. All of my metaphors involve bodies. I imagine my friend climbing a splitter hand-crack that doesn't top out. I picture Barney doing the jitterbug in the clouds. Will my father rise to the sound of the trumpet? So many questions, my heart says to my brain. Some we can't know the answer to, and love is the answer to the rest of them. Shut up and dance, my heart says. Make a joyful noise.

Rapture

IN MY TEENAGE years, in Flagstaff, Arizona, I sometimes attended a church characterized by a certain kind of behavior that I used to call "spirit-filled." The idea was to be inhabited by God. Lifted up, carried away. In those days, I wanted—more than anything—to be given the gift of tongues. The church was located in the Monte Vista Hotel and was separated by a thin partition from the Monte Vista Lounge, a bar with red Naugahyde couches, pool tables, cowboys, bikers, college kids, and hippies. It made for interesting vocal juxtapositions: "Thank you, Jesus! Maranatha! Praise you, Lord!" would ring out from our side of the divide, and in the next moment, from the other side, the smack of pool balls followed by muffled obscenities. It may never actually have happened, but in my memory I hear outbursts like "Hallelujah, motherfucker!" In hindsight, I see people looking for rapture on both sides of the curtain; perhaps we all want to be lifted up, carried away. I thought it meant to meet Jesus in the clouds. Those on the other side of the curtain sought rapture just as earnestly but down a different path.

At the age of fourteen, my greatest fear was of missing the Rapture—the name believers give to the extraordinary moment in which Christ would sweep his righteous followers up in the twinkling of an eye to meet them in the clouds and whisk them away to heaven. Those who were left behind would have a rather rough time of it. They would have to suffer through the Great Tribulation—a period during which Satan and his minions would rule the earth, and people would die in a variety of gruesome ways. Although it's not clear to me now how the pieces of my eschatology fit together, I must have thought that there was a way for people who missed the Rapture to redeem themselves by holding firm to their beliefs in the dark days of the Antichrist. Plan B, so to speak. And so I practiced for plan B on my way home from school.

Play, as coaches are fond of telling us, is preparation for life. So I made up a game. By taking a circuitous route, I tried to make it from school to home without being seen. I flirted with the boundary between woods and houses, crossing a few roads here and there, and sprinting the few unavoidable sections that had no cover of trees or bushes. The goal was simple enough: make it the mile home without being apprehended by the Antichrist's secret police, who, if they caught me, would torture me, try to force me to reveal the location and membership of house churches, and brand the number 666 on my forehead. The rules of the game were a bit more fluid; in general, if anyone acknowledged my presence, I lost. It was a bit trickier with oncoming cars. If I darted for cover before they were too close, I considered myself hidden. If a car turned a corner and faced me head-on, all was lost. If I lost the game too soon, I changed the rules in my favor. My method was to flit from tree to tree, or woodpile, or rock, seeing but not being seen. The easiest part of the journey was the section where I could go up into the Ponderosa forest and follow a dirt road that paralleled a gas pipeline. The hardest parts were closest to home and school—inhabited landscape. Of course, the game didn't begin until I was far enough away from school to not be observed behaving oddly by other students. I may have been an earnest believer, unashamed of the Lord, but I still didn't want anyone to notice what I was doing. To be branded an idiot by my peers was worse than being branded by the Antichrist.

The price of being caught by the secret police was high. I vividly imagined an array of torture techniques they would use on me to get me to reveal the location of home churches, the few remaining cells of believers who had somehow missed the Rapture and had to stand firm in the face of persecution and martyrdom. I was not at all confident that I could withstand these tortures. Would I betray my Lord and family if, for instance, they buried me up to my neck next to a red anthill and then poured honey in my ears, eyes, nostrils, and mouth? Would I curse the name of Jesus if they put my testicles in a vise and slowly crushed them? What if they used a cattle prod? What if they captured someone I loved—say, my brother—and threatened to do one of these things to him unless I told them what they wanted to know? When I honestly considered the likely level of my resolve, I shuddered. Better to win the game and get home unnoticed.

On one occasion, I saw a pickup truck on the pipeline road. This was unusual; the rough road was nearly always empty. I darted into the woods and hid behind a clump of cliffrose, waiting for Satan's minions to pass. To my dismay, the truck didn't pass. It stopped, right by my hiding place. Had I been seen? My pulse quickened. Actually, the game sort of melted into real life, and I wondered if I had really been seen and if I was about to encounter some trouble. The events that unfolded, then, would stick in my memory as vividly as any imagined torture. I had not been seen; in fact, the truck's passengers were certain of their isolation, which is why they stopped the truck. A boy and a girl, a couple of years older than me. High schoolers. From my dusty, scratchy vantage point under a bush, I saw them hustle, in the grip of some urgency, to the bed of the pickup, while the boy was unbuttoning his Levi's. He sat on the tailgate and the girl knelt before him. I forgot all about the Lord, and it didn't even take a cattle prod.

I longed for the Rapture. Not only did I want to be lifted up and carried away—I wanted it for everyone I knew. In those days I thought that rapture happened to the ones who held on to the right formula. I was afraid my friends might miss the Rapture too, and this led me to engage in annoying and even illegal acts of evangelism. Later, it led me to seminary, where I banged my head against the sacred walls, trying to understand grace against a backdrop of rules and doctrines and contradictory Bible verses. I grew up, got married, had a daughter, and worked a range of jobs from firefighter to fisherman to teacher to group home manager for a household of developmentally disabled men. Through it all, I was still waiting for an outward sign of an inner transformation. Still waiting for the gift of tongues, you might say. It never came.

Eventually, my rope of certainties ran out. To make a long story short: in just a few months, both my marriage and my church unraveled. I began to feel a pretty strong dissonance between who I thought I ought to be and who I was turning out to be. I tried to hang on to doctrines, but I felt them slipping away. To help myself stay grounded, I went on hunting trips with a man I had always considered "righteous and spirit-filled," but I increasingly found that I couldn't talk to him about much of anything except elk and God. It turned out to be not enough to talk about.

I was surrounded by people who mattered to me, but I wasn't sure—not really sure—that I was one of them. I felt like an imposter in my own life. I tried to make sense of the issues that were dividing the church: the role of women, the inclusion of homosexuals, the literal interpretation of scripture. My best friends at the time were traditional and orthodox, suspicious of the waves of change that were sweeping through the congregation. (The women's prayer group had read *Women Who Run with the Wolves*. The men were scared of them. I think I was scared of them.)

As my marriage crumbled, I remember crying in my garden, feeling disconsolate after ripping out the dead peas and the spent tomatoes. I left my wife's house and lived in sin with a woman who had a rocky relationship with the church and a good relationship with wine, trouble, and laughter. She had been in the church for decades, coming to it in the heyday of the Jesus People movement years before I came along, but had always been a bit of a black sheep. She was given to irreverent inclinations and possessed a wonderfully wicked sarcastic wit. She loved jazz, fishing, skinny-dipping, and the wind blowing through her hair on road trips. She was schooled by the nuns of St. Ursula's in the tough town of Great Falls, Montana. For these reasons, and others, I liked her.

I had also heard that she had the gift of tongues. One morning as we were making scrambled eggs, I asked her about it. "Oh yes," she said. It was quite a moment for me; I was in the presence of . . . well, something. Was it rapture? "Could you do it?" I asked. "Can you do it for me now?" I was sort of kidding. I had always had the understanding that one couldn't decide to do that sort of thing, that it "came upon you" when God deemed you worthy or the moment ripe. But I'll be damned if she didn't start spouting Holy Ghost Language four inches from my face, as if it was no big deal. She could speak in tongues, all right. She could turn it off and on like a faucet. She proved it to me over bacon and eggs, after I had spent the night with her in sin. It was impressive, I must admit. But also, somehow, ordinary. Something shifted in me, and I knew, quite suddenly, that it didn't mean a thing. (The gift of tongues I mean—not the night of sin.)

Except for funerals, I haven't darkened the doorway of a church for many years now. These days, the mountains are my church. They are, for one thing, much quieter. Above timberline, there is stillness rather than babbling, and when I enter into that stillness I can begin to listen to my own soul, to look for my own answers down my own path. When I enter into the stillness, I don't feel like an imposter, and I don't need to know the answers to every question. I'm not sure if it's rapture that I feel in the mountains. If it is, then it is a quiet, deep, still kind of rapture—not like sexual excitement or religious fervor.

I remember a particular day in the North Cascades of Washington State that shines in my memory like a jewel. In some ways it was a typical day, like many others, and so it carries with it the sacredness of the familiar rather than the exotic. Why it stands out in my memory, perhaps, is that it was during a particularly rough time in my life. I was stumbling in my second marriage, I couldn't find good work, I felt inadequate as a parent—in general my confidence and joy were at a low ebb, while my sense of failure and inarticulate resentment were rather high. I was going to the mountains, I guess you might say, to be lifted up and carried away.

I was headed for the Stuart Range, a splendid outlier of jagged granite peaks on the eastern flank of the Cascades. My plan was a one-day traverse of the upper Enchantment Basin peaks: Dragontail, the Witches Tower, Little Annapurna, and Enchantment. The climbing wasn't technical, but the elevation gain was prodigious and the effort involved substantial. It would be a long day in the mountains. I would make a circuit across the Upper Enchantment Basin—a stark and barren rolling upland of white granite, snow, wildflowers, golden larches, and lakes. This time of year, the lakes would be frozen and the meadows covered by undulating waves of eye-numbing whiteness.

I set out from the trailhead at about three in the morning, making my way through the woods with a headlamp. At about 4:30 a hint of light on one side of the sky told me where the sun would rise. I startled something, maybe a bear, that crashed through the underbrush. The typical predawn downslope wind rushed through the Icicle Creek watershed, chilling the sweat on my neck and making me shiver. Then I made my way up switchbacks, a lot of them. Just as the sun broke over the horizon, I arrived at Colchuck Lake, still frozen, beneath the broad, craggy north faces of Dragontail and Colchuck Peak catching the salmon-colored fire of dawn. That's when the work started. A heavy snowpack meant deep snow even in June, and I post-holed my way around the lake and started to step-kick in the long snow chutes that led up to Aasgard Pass and the upper basin.

It was a stiff climb up Aasgard Pass, step-kicking into the crusty snow and scrambling between heathery benches and granite outcrops. The sun got higher; the lake below got smaller. On the final slope up Dragontail, the snow turned to mush in the growing heat of the day. My ears buzzed. To my right, the sheer north face of Dragontail dropped off for two thousand feet. To my left, the moor-like expanse of Enchantment Basin rolled down to the splendid granite prow of Prusik Peak.

On the summit of Dragontail, I sat down for a meal of greasy pepperoni and half-melted cheddar cheese on rye crackers, but while cutting the pepperoni with my pocketknife I deeply sliced into the notch between my thumb and index finger. I wrapped the wound as well as I could and finished my meal. Perhaps from exertion, or loss of blood, or the dazzling whiteness of snowfields, dots danced before my eyes. I felt unnaturally light. I looked out at the sea of jagged peaks, the sharply defined north ridge of Mount Stuart etched against a cobalt sky. The looming dome of Mount Rainier seemed to float somewhere between this world and the next. I felt the impulse to offer praise, but I didn't vocalize it. One of the joys of long mountain days is the opportunity to be in prolonged silence.

I visited several summits, each one splendid. Finally, it was time to leave. I glissaded down narrow snow chutes, paying close attention to my feet, lest I hit a rock or a dimple and snowball for a thousand feet to the banks of Colchuck Lake. Once down, I tried to shave off some distance by taking a shortcut across the frozen lake that turned out to be not so frozen. After an hour's rest on a flat boulder, stark naked while my clothes could become if not dry then at least a little less wet I made my way around the lake, post-holing to my hips in treacherous early-summer snow. Finally reaching a trail, I began to trudge the final five miles to my car. It seemed to take forever. I fell into a plodding rhythm defined by the recurrent squelching of wet shoes. With each mile and each thousand-foot drop in elevation, the temperature rose until the day was scorching. By the time I reached my car—fourteen hours and twenty miles after leaving it—I was parched and exhausted. I plunged my head into the icy waters of Icicle Creek. Spray from the cascading water split sunlight into slivers of rainbow. I stripped out of my damp clothes, put on some dry shorts, found a sandy patch between granite boulders along a turbulent stretch of creek, and fell almost instantly asleep. When I woke, I couldn't remember where I was, how I got there, or what was supposed to happen next.

There was only the rush of the creek, the wind through pines, and a sky blue enough to swim into. It is how I imagine transitioning into the next world.

EARWORM

_____

THIS STORY BEGINS in the dark, under a night sky. Stars were thick as fuzz on a peach, the cool mountain air redolent with alpine scents, and Swamp Creek filled the darkness with the sound of its single-minded love affair with gravity. It was three thirty in the morning, and I was about to strap on my headlamp and begin my ascent of Tomyhoi Peak, one of the many fine summits along the border between Washington and Canada, in a steep and rugged part of the Cascades known as the Chilliwack Peaks. On the long drive up from Seattle, I had listened to my iPod: the Rolling Stones, Tab Benoit, Pearl Jam. As I got closer to my destination, I traded rock 'n' roll for music more acoustic and contemplative: Nickel Creek, Yo-Yo Ma. Finally, in keeping with the landscape, I played a collection of Norwegian folk songs as I made my way up the bumpy forest road. The songs were haunting, lovely, and sparse. They reminded me of pebbles on the bed of a clear mountain stream. They were a perfect segue into the silence that would characterize the rest of the day. Or so I hoped.

One of the pleasures of long days spent alone in the mountains is the opportunity to experience extended periods of silence. Or, more precisely, near silence. There are often subtle noises—the rustling of small creatures, water, wind. I was accompanied by the sound of my own breathing as I hoofed it up switchbacks through the primeval darkness of dense western hemlock and Douglas fir.

My feet made a satisfying chopping sound as I kicked steps in snow-banks hardened by the morning chill. Gradually ridgetops became outlined against the brightening eastern sky. Perhaps the most beautiful sound was that of running water—the countless rivulets and the larger streams tumbling down the steep escarpment of Yellow Aster Butte toward their confluence with the Nooksack River.

It was to be a good and simple day. I was at peace with the toads that were inexplicably numerous, hopping indolently across the trail. And I was at peace with the mysterious creatures of the night that are never seen and only heard, crashing through alder thickets. I was at peace with the ptarmigan that hooted as they skittered through hummocks of heather. And although it might make me a bit nervous to see a mountain lion as I did on a previous trip up Tomyhoi Peak, if I did, I intended to be at peace with it as well.

Hours passed, and miles. I persistently gained altitude, moving out of the deep forest and into meadows where the mountain hemlock and subalpine fir were smaller and scattered. I entered the domain of wildflowers: deep blue lupine, buttery asters, crimson shooting star, snowy tufts of beargrass, purple heather, and humble glacier lilies, their yellow heads bowed down. As I traversed the flank of Yellow Aster Butte, blueberries carpeted the slopes with delicate green. When the sun finally rose, it was as if the top of Mount Baker was on fire. The salmon-colored flame slowly spread down the slopes. Rounding the butte's shoulder, I descended into a rolling basin of meadows, granite outcrops, snowbanks, and about a dozen small bodies of water, ranging in size from tent-sized tarns to something that might be called a lake. Some of these were still frozen; some were clear and smooth as glass, with a tinge of turquoise where the water was deepest. Scattered groves of subalpine fir clustered on top of a few of the more prominent nobs, but the terrain was generally alpine tundra. A braided waterfall marked the abrupt end of the basin as it plunged into a cleft on its way to the valley floor below.

After a break at the highest of the lakes, where I finished off a loaf of crusty peasant bread and a pepperoni, I shouldered my pack and picked my way through a boulder field toward an unrelentingly steep slope. Beyond the reach of maintained trails, the way was simply up. The slope was the admission price for my favorite part of the trip, the heathery benches on the south ridge of Tomyhoi Peak. It is fair to say that this is a sacred place to me. I have long loved this place and have returned to it when I sought out this kind of peace and silence. The tarns in the basin below shimmered in the morning sun. As I gained altitude, a sea of peaks made themselves visible, rolling away in all directions. It was like seeing old friends after a long absence. In my mind, I named all of the peaks, and noted that I had climbed most of them. And then a thought occurred to me. It seemed innocent enough at the time, but it was to bear bitter fruit. The thought was this: *I'd like to climb every mountain.*

And that is all it took. By the time I realized I was singing, it was too late. It always is.

Some songs, like pebbles in a clear stream, are refreshing to the soul. Others masquerade as if they're refreshing to the soul but, in fact, lead to madness. The most deranged earworms of all are those songs that are supposed to be inspiring. If Lucifer pretends to be an angel of light, then his songs pretend to, as they say, "lift the spirit." I was in the grip of such a song. In a particularly cruel twist, the song's final phrase—*till you find your dream*—turns out not to be final at all, but merely the occasion for a key change. The diabolical anthem mocks the very act of climbing, refusing to end, forever stretching upward as you search in vain for your elusive dream. As I ascended Tomyhoi Peak, I felt like Dante descending into the Inferno, and with each step farther into hell, another key change upward.

I don't know how long this went on. Neither do I know how I finally banished the song from my inner ear, but eventually, blessedly, as I sat upon a flat stone on the peak's first false summit, I realized that I was free of it. But it would have been better had I not realized it, for as soon as I did—as soon as I listened carefully and heard only silence and then foolishly congratulated myself—the truth of Scripture made itself manifest: "When an evil spirit comes out of a man, it goes through arid places seeking rest and does not find it. Then it says, 'I will return to the house I left.' When it arrives, it finds the house swept clean and put in order. Then it goes and takes seven other spirits more wicked than itself, and they go and live there. And the final condition of that man is worse than the first."

It is hard to say which song from *The Sound of Music* is the worst, but for the next five hours, all of them took up residence in my noggin. I think each of them is worse than all the others.

The summit was sublime. Hundreds of peaks, some of them burnished copper in the sunlight, others in silhouette. Across the deep cleft of the Tomyhoi Creek watershed, the rugged cliffs of American Border Peak and Canadian Border Peak carved the horizon. Beyond them, the even more imposing Mount Slesse, like a great fang jutting into the sky. To the south, the queen of the range, Mount Baker, draped in ice, her glaciers ruffled by seracs and crevasses. Perhaps most impressive of all, the complex and looming north face of Mount Shuksan, with its hanging glaciers, forbidding towers, and perfect summit pyramid piercing a thin, lenticular cloud. I would have enjoyed it even more had my head not been shrieking "tiiiiiiill yooooouuu fiiiiiiiinnnd yoooouur dreeeeeaaaaam!" In a sudden flash of insight, I knew that I was capable of violence.

Understand that I have nothing against nuns. At various times in my life, I have been profoundly moved by the words of St. Theresa of Avila, the visions of Hildegard of Bingen, and the work of Dorothy Day. I once spent a wonderful weekend at the convent of Our Lady of the Rock, enjoying the company of the kind sisters and their shaggy Scottish Highland cattle. But if, at that very moment, a nun had been standing before me on the precipitous summit of Tomyhoi, I would have pushed her off without hesitation.

MOUNT ELDEN

IN MY MEMORY, Flagstaff, Arizona, is forever stuck somewhere in the 1970s.

Linda Vista was the edge of town, and beyond it, the woods. Because a mountain requires some degree of modesty, to preserve the sense of mystery, Mount Elden did not rise directly from town. An apron of forest skirted the mountain's southern flank, and this forest was my childhood playground, my refuge.

It is a handsome forest of ponderosa pine, cliffrose, the occasional Gambel oak, and other high desert shrubbery like mountain mahogany. I remember tall pithy stalks of mullein that we used to do battle. The botanical swords fell apart in a sticky, fuzzy mess.

The first spanking I ever received—I must have been about six years old—was for wandering off into the woods alone. My father asked me where I had been, and I said "around." Which was not a lie.

Halfway to the mountain's base was the pipeline road. Along certain segments of the road, you could sometimes hear a strange percussive sound that had something to do with the natural gas line. As kids, we had our own mythology: the thumping sound was the heartbeat of a murdered girl who was rumored to be buried somewhere between the road and the mountain.

We knew all the bike paths that wound through the ponderosas and the cliffrose. I remember a tree fort in a Gambel oak, with an alarm system that consisted of a makeshift chute down which we would roll acorns into a coffee can. The alarm meant "someone is coming, hide the *Playboy*."

I don't remember how old we were when Dave Helm and I found some pottery pieces laying on the ground in a nondescript location. We dug a bit, and found more. Eventually we had two pits about three feet across and a few feet deep. We got a lot of pottery shards out of those pits. I think now that we had found a spot that would have been of interest to archaeologists, but as kids I doubt we had any inkling that adults might have an interest in that pottery. The woods were the domain of kids.

But more than the forest above Linda Vista, it was the southern slope of Mount Elden itself that I loved, with its jumbled pile of dacite boulders and its interconnecting maze of tunnels, caves, and ramps. I loved both the sense of intimacy that could be found on a single ledge and the complexity of how each ledge was connected to other ledges. There were secret places, bats, niches that were always warm even in winter, or nooks that were always cold even in summer.

When I was about ten, the boundary of Linda Vista—which I had always taken for granted—was breached. I didn't take it well.

A swath of forest was cleared, and it seemed that a large building was on the way. At dusk, when no one was around, I pulled out all the surveyor's stakes and threw them into the woods, and then with my foot I erased all the white chalk lines.

About a week later, the lines and stakes had reappeared. Once again, I uprooted the stakes and erased the lines. This time I happened to find the bag of chalk on the construction site, and I laid new lines in the wrong places, hoping to confuse the construction crew.

Soon, right above Steves Street, houses were under construction. I went to these, also at dusk, and threw a stone through every single window of every single house.

No matter; the windows were replaced, and people moved into the houses. My delinquency was to no avail. The large building became a church, and I think all the walls were in the right places. The boundaries of town continued to encroach on Mount Elden.

Sometime in junior high, I got hold of 150 feet of fraying gold line and tried to use it. Dave Helm was my first climbing partner, and I think we learned by trial and error. The only knot we knew was the bowline: a rabbit going around the tree into a hole.

It was in the days before sticky rubber shoes and harnesses. We floundered, scorched our hips with bad hip belays, crushed our testicles with awkward body rappels, and pretended we knew what to do with stoppers and hexes. Mostly we rappelled and top-roped.

If my memory is correct, Dave and I and Chuck Curry were camping somewhere near the band of cliffs that bisects the mountain's two main lobes, due north of about Tindle Street. Under our superb tutelage, Chuck was rappelling for the first time. He was having some trouble committing to that first step over the cliff edge, so Dave and I encouraged him by lobbing gooey blobs of oatmeal at him. *Splat. Splat.*

In high school, Dave and I graduated to West Elden, where most Flagstaff boys and girls learn to climb. The names of those climbs still linger in my mind: the Prow, Flip & Grunt, the Meatgrinder, the Face, the Idaho Flake.

Once, after top-roping some nameless crack, one of us—I can't remember who—leaned against the dead tree we had used as an anchor, then jumped away as the tree abruptly gave way and toppled over the cliff edge. We peered over the edge, then at each other. "Whoa! Shit!" It was a good first lesson in evaluating anchors more carefully.

I know it sounds sentimental, but I have often felt that mountains were friends. Of course in one way this is silly, because a mountain doesn't care if I exist, or if I fall to my death because I used a dead tree as an anchor. But the mountains give me a sense of well-being, and they hold memories for me. Mount Elden is the oldest of my mountain friends.

The close proximity of people has been hard on the mountain, especially in terms of fire. This year, the Schultz fire ravaged the landscape between Mount Elden and the peaks. Like many of us, I remember the mountain going up in flames in the Radio Fire of 1977.

I went up to the lookout not long after the Radio fire. Just as on most other occasions, the first notable sound was the wind. But it seemed different, threading its way through charred trees. Still, even the mountain's bare bones held a kind of severe yet elegant grace.

But why did the trees look orange? The charcoal trunks seemed to be mottled with a blotchy orange lichen of some sort. It also seemed that a lot of insects were swarming around the trees.

When I got closer, I could see that the orange splotches were colonies of ladybugs. Millions of them. They formed huge rafts, clinging to each other and to the burned wood.

Ladybug, ladybug, fly away home; your house is on fire . . .

At that time I didn't know that this is common after a wildfire. In future years, I would see it in the mountains of Idaho and Nevada while working on fire crews. At the time, it just seemed like a strange bit of magic that came to bless the sad, bald head of Mount Elden.

SNOWFALL AND BRIMSTONE

In the winter of 1986, I was living in a cabin a few miles outside of Fairbanks, Alaska. I had no car, but I had a good parka, a beaver pelt hat, and Sorels for my feet, so I didn't mind hitchhiking to Anchorage for a weekend to visit my friends Mary Barber and her daughter Debbie Barber McDonald. Debbie was vastly pregnant, and her husband Mike was working up at Prudhoe Bay in the oil fields. I thought I might get to meet a brand-new baby. It seemed like a fun adventure for my twenty-fourth birthday.

Getting a ride down was not a problem. Hitchhikers in Alaska—at least in those days, and particularly in winter—rarely had to wait long. It was more than three hundred miles to Anchorage, but I lucked out and got a ride almost all the way to Debbie's house. We had a great visit and spoke with affection and humor of Mary's son and Debbie's younger brother, Danny, who had recently died in an airplane crash. The next morning, at about 4:00 a.m., I drove Mary and Debbie down icy streets to Providence hospital, where she gave birth to a baby girl just fifteen minutes after we got there. Later that day, it was time to go back home. I said good-bye to my friends as they dropped me off near Eagle River, and I was on my way.

Soon a light snowfall started. Then it got heavier. The snow seemed wrong somehow. Just a little bit gray and greasy between the fingers. Walking along the highway, I had no idea that Mount

Augustine, a volcano in Cook Inlet, had erupted. The greasy snow was ash. To be more precise, it was a blend of snow and ash. I learned the true nature of the greasy snow from the first driver to pick me up, a man who was an Alaska State landfill inspector. I had never thought of that job before, but I guess somebody has to do it. For the next couple of hours, I followed him through hills and valleys of garbage as he enlightened me regarding what a landfill inspector actually looks for among the old refrigerators and moldy magazines. Alas, I can't remember those things now. I vaguely recall that he "measured" things. Gases? Volumes? Density? I don't know. After two landfills, he decided to call it a day. Time to go home. He was concerned about driving in ashfall, which can be rough on an internal combustion engine.

He left me in Wasilla. I was wondering if my luck was going to get sparse, given that not many people would be driving during an eruption. As it turned out, not everyone knew the snow was something more than snow, and the next driver to pull over for me, in a battered purple truck, didn't have a working radio. He reached across the cab to open the door for me, and I hopped in, grateful. The first thing I noticed was a grin that seemed one part cheerfulness and one part something more sinister. The second thing I noticed was a livid purple scar—to match the truck, perhaps—that traveled from one ear, down along his chin, and up to the other ear. I was still in a stage of life where I applied the word *interesting* to people who are more accurately described as *dangerous*. Besides, I needed a ride. It was winter in Alaska, and I was a long way from my cabin. Albeit gently, brimstone was falling. It turned out I was riding with a principal drug dealer of the Bristol Bay region of Alaska. At least that's what the man claimed, and I had no reason to doubt him. His scar seemed like a valid résumé. While rural and roadless, Bristol Bay during fishing season is awash in money and reckless young men—a good place for a drug dealer. He bragged about how much money he made, how many fishing boats and tenders waited for his deliveries.

I didn't understand why we stopped at several mini-mart payphones, and my driver kept making very short calls before getting back in the truck, chuckling. While trying not to appear too nosy, I mentioned how curiously short all the phone calls were. "So they can't be traced," is all the man said. A little while later he added, "I'm baiting the cops." I have no idea if he really was, but he seemed like a guy who might. I was starting to wonder if riding with this guy was such a good idea.

Outside of Wasilla, daylight dwindled along with any signs of human habitation. I was heading north into the arctic heart of darkness with a sort of gleeful Alaska Bush version of Kurtz. We soon escaped the greasy snow; the ashfall didn't reach as far north as Willow, where we stopped and got burgers. He began to tell me about his homestead, which was somewhere near Cantwell, the last little outpost before the highway cut through the dramatic wilderness of the Alaska Range. He enthusiastically invited me to spend the night at his cabin, where he had plenty of weed and brew. Something in his gaze warned me that there were other unspoken and unsavory aspects to this invitation.

I weighed my options. The farther we got from Anchorage, the more traffic dwindled. The distance between Cantwell and Nenana, the next town, was about a hundred miles, and I couldn't imagine anyone making the trip in the middle of a winter night and during an eruption. It seemed like Purple Scar Man was the last likely bet for a ride, until tomorrow. It would be a walk of who-knows-how-long, on a winter night. I didn't know how cold it was, but it was certainly subzero.

It was also an easy choice. I had already imagined several ways in which the night could go drastically wrong if I opted for the security of a warm cabin. I wanted to lose neither my life nor my virginity in this fashion on my twenty-fourth birthday. When we got to Cantwell, I hopped out of the truck and abruptly announced that I was continuing on foot. There was a testy moment of silence—a moment in which I wondered if some quick and surreptitious violence might ensue—before Purple Scar Man said, simply, "Suit yourself." Then he sped away to his cabin among the spindly black spruce.

I walked relieved through the crunchy snow for several hours. Far north of Augustine's plume, the sky was clear. In the utter silence, I imagined (or did I?) that the aurora overhead was making tiny, crisp, tinkling sounds. Spears of emerald, then a weaving curtain, and then a series of magenta patches skipped across the sky like flat stones on a pond. I didn't have a watch, but not a single car appeared for four or five hours. I suspected that the eruption kept drivers at home. A wolf pack filled the void—first one long, rising, piercingly beautiful howl followed by a chorus of yips and glissandos, at times discordant and at times converging into what seemed like intentional resolution.

The cold was not extreme. I guessed it was holding steady at about minus ten, for which I was more than adequately dressed. Finally a pair of headlights appeared across the tundra. They seemed to be visible for a very long time, growing in amplitude almost imperceptibly. It was a big rig, the kind with a bed behind the cab and a bear gun on the bed. The driver seemed perplexed to find me but glad for the company. He took me all the way to Fairbanks, sharing recipes for wild game along the way.

What Is Not Seen

I. **I can still** feel the rocking of the *Sea Bear* as I leaned too far over her gunwale, slashing madly, stupidly with my gaffe at the imperturbable water. Gone, *gone!* The biggest king salmon I will ever see. Or, to be more precise, the biggest king salmon that I will ever not quite see but will believe in with the faith we reserve for things not seen. A wave of self-pity overwhelmed me. Once again, I slashed at the water with my gaffe. *Fuck, Fuck, Fucketty-fuck, Fuck!!!*

I stared at the rolling billows for a long time.

Just moments earlier, I had seen the persistent yank on the line. I didn't know, yet, if it was a salmon, a halibut, a toothsome ling-cod, or one of the ubiquitous rockfish. Whatever it would turn out to be, a particularly violent tug convinced me that it would be a noteworthy catch. When its sleek, dusky form was close enough to the boat to be momentarily glimpsed, I felt a rush of adrenaline. It was a salmon, and a big one indeed. *Jesus!* I thought. *That might be a seventy-pound fish!* It was my third season fishing, and I thought I could estimate the weight of a salmon by a kink in the line and a fleeting glance at dimpled water. In my previous two seasons, I had not seen, much less caught, a king of such magnitude.

It was my first day out. The day before I had wandered through the harbors of Sitka, Alaska, looking for work. Despite my lack of experience on a troller (I had set-netted for two seasons in a different part of the state), I found a skipper who was willing to take me on, as his fifty-foot boat was difficult to manage by himself. I went home to pack my duffel and then put out to sea on the *Sea Bear*.

I was the only crew. While the skipper was at the wheel, I was in the stern, running hydraulic pulleys that raised and lowered six weighted cables into the water. To each cable, I clipped leads baited with herring. As I raised the cables, a sharp tug on the lead indicated the presence of a halibut, rockfish, lingcod, or a sleek and bright chinook. We were after the kings. It was my job to bring the fish on board, unceremoniously end its life, gut and clean it, then put it on ice. To bring a fish in, I used a gaffe, which is a stick with a metal hook lashed to one end. It may sound strange and perhaps hypocritical, but even as I eviscerated them, I had great admiration for those bright kings—so full of fight, so full of spirit.

I will eschew the overwrought description of great struggle. Suffice it to say that in the moment just before the fish broke the surface of the water, just before I could hook it with my gaffe and hoist it into the stern, in the time it takes for an ego to go from full to flaccid without comprehending the shift, the line went slack and the shadowy creature slipped, without fuss, away. A single chinook of that size is worth a lot of money and a lot of glory. I don't know what galled me more—the fact that I didn't get the fish, or that no one was there to witness the epic saga. No one saw; no one knew.

Oh well, I thought, forlornly, as I gathered myself together and took a deep breath. *Dukkha.* Life is dissatisfaction and struggle. For both me and the salmon. It did not want to die, and for this it cannot be blamed. I got back to work. With the rest of the season still ahead, I tried to hope that a bigger one would come along. But I should have known better than to expect that any fish I caught could be bigger than the one I didn't.

I know, I know. We all have such tales. *Almost caught it.* (Sure you did, Mark. *Almost* partners up late at night with *if only* when we drink red wine at three in the morning on the kitchen floor.) But I'm telling you—it happened. At the time, I didn't even tell the skipper, who had been up in the wheelhouse steering the boat. I didn't want him to doubt me.

Nevertheless, doubt creeps, as it should, into my recollection. I did not, after all, clearly *see* the creature. Was it really such an archetypal fish? I don't know. But in my memory and in my soul, that king of kings still lurks just beneath the surface of my consciousness and just beyond the powers of perception. More real than God, but just as elusive, unpredictable, and unprovable. Maybe it is what we cannot see that leaves the greatest mark upon us.

II. **AFTER FISHING SEASON** ended, the autumn days grew short, and the rains settled in. Soon, mist shrouded the rocky islands, and November gales ripped through branches of mountain hemlock and Sitka spruce. What fell as rain on the coast, fell as wet, heavy snow in the mountains. I assumed that brown bears were hibernating.

Even in the winter, I love to climb mountains. It is a way for me to find peace and hear my own thoughts over the clutter of daily life. So on a windy November day, I set out for the summit of a mountain on the outskirts of Sitka. I worked my way through fresh, heavy snow until I was a few hundred feet below the summit.

Crossing a small clearing, I came upon a bear's paw print. It was enormous, maybe the diameter of a soccer ball. The outline of the print was crisp and distinct; it had not yet been rendered fuzzy by the light, powdery snow that was falling. Indeed, it seemed that the print still glistened from the heat of the body that had made it.

My pulse quickened. I scoured the landscape, looking for the bear. I had no doubt that it was very close. I also had no doubt that it knew where I was and probably had known for quite a while. The tracks angled off into the woods to my right. The squirrely wind had no discernable consistent direction, so I couldn't tell if I was upwind or downwind.

Eventually, I had to decide what to do. I continued to climb, since that was what I had come to do in the first place, and I doubted that the bear shared this objective. Floundering through deep fluff, I made my way to the summit, where a fierce wind drove snow snakes over the ridge. A storm was brewing. The charcoal sky blended into the impenetrable gray of the Pacific Ocean. I knew I should waste no time getting down, but I took a moment to fully feel the peculiar mix of uneasiness and joy. On the way down, I knew that the inscrutable, invisible bear was somewhere in the trees, not sleeping.

I've seen big bears. I've encountered them in the wild, although never at close range, and I've never been threatened by one. I've heard many stories about their power, and I've seen that power myself. Once, from a small plane, I watched a magnificent blonde sow gallop as fast as a racehorse through swampy muskeg. It is hard to walk, much less run, through such country. The bear, running from the plane, came to a thirty-degree slope. Charging up the hill, she didn't slow down one whit. If anything, she accelerated. When I think of power, I see that bear in my mind's eye. But I've never felt the presence of a bear as acutely as on that November day when I could not see the animal, but knew it to be present.

In addition to being a fisherman, my skipper on the *Sea Bear* also worked as a hunting guide in Tongass National Forest. His primary targets were enormous brown bears, and his primary clients were rich white men. He was a successful guide, and he usually guided his customers to their quarry. I was saddened to think of those magnificent bears reduced to rugs just to fatten the egos of corporate CEOs and lawyers. (Yet how different am I from those lawyers? I don't know. I certainly wanted to catch that fish.)

I also don't know if my skipper felt regret about killing bears, because I didn't ask him. But I did ask him if there was a particularly memorable bear, perhaps one that returned in his dreams. He said that the bear that lingers in his imagination is one he did not see. One he did not get. One who led him in circles, so that it was unclear who was stalking whom. The one who left my skipper's camp in a shambles, tents shredded, supplies scattered. The one who chewed up his frying pan. I don't know of any single image that conveys a bear's power more vividly than this impression not of a bear, but of a bear's passage: toothmarks—not just scratches, mind you, but deep indentations—in a cast-iron skillet.

III. POWER IS IN a bear's jaws, but power is also in small things: the steady drip that wears away granite, or the mushroom that breaks through asphalt. The most aware I've ever been that I was at the mercy of another creature in the wild was not due to a bear or any other top-of-the-food-chain predator. I was humbled by a common insect.

Several years before I lived in Sitka, I spent a summer farther north, near Kotzebue. I was headed for the coast to help a friend set-net for salmon. We started out upriver, at his home near the village of Ambler, on the banks of the Kobuk River. We were at Ambler when we celebrated the Fourth of July. We water-skied on the river, then sat around wondering what else do to. Someone got the idea to head up to an abandoned jade mine about ten miles away in the foothills of the Brooks Range. At about midnight, four young men departed from the village. It was a spur-of-the-moment adventure. We didn't take much. We had a gun, of course, but I don't remember if anyone mentioned mosquitoes.

We rode four-wheelers as far as we could go, then set out on foot across the tundra. It was slow going through dense thickets of willow, over uneven hummocks of berries and heather, and through the occasional pit of boot-sucking muck. Even at its lowest point in the sky, the arctic sun was hot, and our shirts were drenched in sweat. The mosquitoes, bad enough along the Kobuk, became unbearable out on the tundra. I had never seen anything like the swarms that completely covered our backs, necks, faces, and arms.

Several times, we slathered on the DEET. It didn't keep the insects off of us, but at least it kept them from draining us dry of blood. We swatted them with bandanas, but it was like trying to bail out a sinking boat with a teaspoon. I felt that the incessant whine and the constant biting were going to drive me insane. My friends, arctic veterans, seemed to hold up better than me, but after a while they showed the strain as well. We stopped and brought out the bottle of DEET. It was almost empty. And we were a long ways from any refills.

Laughter, as we looked at the very small amount of repellent left in the bottle and considered how far it would go among four grown men who, between them, had a substantial amount of exposed skin. I don't recall if anything was said, but it seemed like we looked at each other with the same kind of grim amusement that might pass between four sailors on a raft out at sea, just before they must decide who will go overboard.

We did the best we could. The bug dope didn't amount to much. I don't know what anyone else was thinking, but I was wondering how far it was back to the village. I was also wondering how long it would take for a human body to be drained of blood. But we didn't turn around; instead, we pressed on toward the mine. Being up the slope of the mountain, at least the mine might have a breeze and offer some respite from the ruthless insects.

In a moment of quiet, I listened. Perhaps I imagined it, but it seemed that the familiar whine of the mosquitoes, magnified by billions or trillions, had a deeper resonance, a hum like electricity going through high voltage power lines. I realized that I was not worried about the mosquitoes I could see. The swarm was prodigious, but it was comprehensible. No, it was the mosquitoes I could not see that humbled me and held my fate in their . . . well, not hands. Probosci? As far as I could see, and farther . . . for hundreds of miles, in every direction, mosquitoes as dense as this. The gun was of no use.

Luck smiled on us. In a few more miles, we reached the mine, and—as is often the case with such places—it had a cache of unopened crates of things like corned beef hash, pilot bread and jam, and . . . mosquito repellent.

IV. WHEN I FIRST came to Alaska, when I was young and stupid, when my ambition exceeded my caution, when my confidence far outweighed my experience, and when I took it for granted that my cup of luck was refilled every morning, I climbed a mountain in the Chugach Range. It was a minor peak, probably unnamed, really just a subsidiary bump along a corniced ridge, but it looked over a glorious valley.

It was late afternoon on an April day. On my way up the mountain, limbs of willow and alder were sheathed in tiny blades of frost, catching and splintering the cold brilliance of the early spring sun. Nearing the crest of the ridge, I was awed by the layering of light: salmon-tinged clouds above golden rocky outcrops above milky-blue snow in the shadowed valley.

I wanted to look down into that valley, so I slowly light-footed it toward the edge. The snow upon which I walked was crunchy, firm, and elegantly furrowed and fluted by nearly constant wind. At least it felt firm. Born and raised in the desert Southwest, I was new to the mountains of the north. I didn't fully appreciate the danger of cornices. I didn't understand that under the crusty top layer of snow was a layer about as consolidated as Styrofoam packing peanuts, and that under that was another thin crust, and under that—nothing but air.

Before I knew what was happening, the crust gave way like a trapdoor. My stomach lurched into my throat. Quicker than thought, adrenaline flooded my body. Instinctively, I splayed my arms.

Sometimes there are signs when these things are about to happen, but I didn't yet know how to read them. I was not attuned to the language of snow—the muffled *whump!* that precedes a separating slab or the delicate shift that precedes a sudden snap over a twinkling of loose sugary crystals.

There are some physical sensations a person doesn't forget. One such sensation is to have your body punch through a surface that you thought was solid and to feel your legs swing freely in a space you can't see. It is a sensation I don't care to repeat, but I confess that the recollection of it is enough to remind me how much I love my life and wish it to continue.

Why did the snow give way at precisely the spot that it did? Why did the shelf of snow remain strong enough under my elbows to allow me to crawl out? I'm not sure that *why* is a useful question. At any rate, *because I am one lucky dumbshit* is a possible answer. Some people resort to words like *grace, karma, prayer, fate,* and *luck* to address such questions. Some impute motive to unseen beings, or see every molecule of the seen and unseen world as infused with intentional spirits.

Others could explain to me the physical properties of snow, and how variables such as my body weight and the time of day affect the ever-changing structure and plasticity of snow crystals. Either way, the snow in its glory seems indifferent to my fate and unburdened by responsibility. It—along with the fish, the bear, the storm, and the mosquito—needs only to be what it is. Interconnected to all other animate and inanimate parts of the world in ways we can only partially understand and predict and often cannot see, we live and die, we eat and sometimes are eaten, and we are often pardoned, irrespective of merit.

I never looked into the abyss. I mantled my way back onto the hard snow, praying it would hold my weight, then scrambled down the windward slope on my hands and knees without even seeing the hole that had nearly ushered me into the next (if there is one) life. *No thank you,* I whispered under my breath to the snow. It did not answer, but it continued to shine even more brightly than before in the rays of the setting sun. Which is, I suppose, a kind of answer.

Eye Contact

———————

I. WHEN I MOVED to Alaska in the summer of 1985, I thought I was ready for anything. As I saw it, I was headed north into possibility and redemptive wilderness. With all my possessions in the back of my pickup and a season's worth of firefighting wages in my wallet, I embraced my future with more confidence than my experience merited. The world seemed a fine place. I assumed others felt the same way about it.

When I picked up the girl just a few miles past the Montana border, I looked forward to pleasant company with another open-hearted traveler. My final destination was Fairbanks, my current location the Canadian Rockies, and my inclination was for some conversation on the journey.

"Don't know where you're going," I said, "but if it's on the way to Alaska, I'll take you there." She got in the truck, but without much enthusiasm. Her manner was skittish. Her clothes were tattered and stained. She looked at me as if I had made her get in. As it turned out, holding a conversation of any kind—pleasant or un—was not happening. She was nervous and guarded, prone to giving cryptic answers to my direct questions. But the road went on and on, my radio didn't work, so eventually I learned some things about her.

She was Canadian but had been roaming around the States for about six months. She had run away from home, but it hadn't worked out well, and now she was running back. Home was a place called Hinton, a small town in Alberta. To be more precise, home was a trailer with a leaky roof, mattresses that smelled of mildew, a father who was often drunk and violent, a mother who had pretty much given up on life, and an uncle who was friendly in all the wrong ways.

She had tried to get out of Hinton, but now she was going back. She felt no joy at the prospect of returning, yet she considered it preferable to whatever had happened in the past six months on the road. She was not forthcoming with details, and I did not press her for any. It was hard for me to understand why she would go back to Hinton, but apparently the dismal home she described was preferable to any future she could imagine.

I had entered Canada with a joyous spirit, but traveling with the girl deflated my mood considerably. The hardest aspect of her company was that she wouldn't relax. She was unrelentingly suspicious, shrinking ever so slightly in her seat in response to any movement on my part, such as reaching into a pack for a snack. My jokes—corny, I'll admit—elicited from her no response at all. I quit making them.

Eventually we had to sleep. I had told her when I picked her up that I didn't stay in motels, and that I usually just found a place in the woods and tossed my bag on the ground. She let me know that she had no money, and sleeping on the ground was fine. So I found a pullout where the highway crossed a creek. There was just enough dusky light to find a bed among the willows.

"This is a good spot," I said, indicating a level and fairly private hollow. I quickly added, "I'll sleep over on the other side of that clump of willows, about ten yards in that direction. Good night." I did not see any point in dragging things out. Before getting into my bag, I thought of something I needed to tell her, so I made my way through the willows to the spot she had spread her bag. I spoke casually, not wanting to increase her anxiety. "Hey," I said. "Don't bring any food into your bag. Not even a cracker. Leave it all in the car, okay? We don't want to invite the bears."

But when I looked up at her face and my gaze met hers, I realized she was not afraid of bears. She backed away—just a stutter-step, but I noticed. The message I had hoped to send in my glance was *Don't be afraid*. I don't know what message she saw instead, but it wasn't that one. What her glance said was *Don't come any closer*. It didn't seem a good time to talk about it. I bid her good night again and crawled into my bag, where I mulled over what I could do to make the next day easier.

In the morning she was red-eyed and ragged. "Sleep okay?" I asked. "No," she answered, with no further explanation. I felt certain she had stayed up all night, eyeing the clump of willows that separated us, alert for any movement that would indicate my approach. I noticed, as she stuffed her sleeping bag into its sack, the glint of a jackknife dropping to the ground. She quickly scooped it up and put it in her coat. I wondered if she had spent the night with that knife clenched in her fist.

Day two was a repeat of day one. Attempts at conversation fell flat under the weight of her fear. I didn't understand why she saw me as a threat. Didn't she realize that if I wanted to do her harm, I would have done so already? Shortly before sunset, an abrupt hissing noise, a cloud of steam, and the loss of power told me that my truck was not going to go any farther. We were far from any town. I opened the hood and tried to diagnose the problem. The girl walked a short distance away and then sat, disconsolate, on a gravel bank beside the road. Aside from my impotent curses, the stones she tossed on to the pavement were the only sound.

It was a time before cell phones. We had only each other. The mountains were impassive and unconcerned. I had blown out a frost plug, and I knew that I had neither the skills nor the tools to fix the truck. Earlier in the day, I had promised the girl that we'd drive straight through to Hinton, even though it meant driving through the night. Though I tried to hide it, it was a promise I resented because I wanted to have a leisurely trip through the Rockies, and I wanted to do some hiking. But clearly she didn't want to spend another night in the willows with a strange man only a few yards away.

Now things had changed. I told her I wasn't able to fix the truck. I'd have to wait for help and then arrange to be towed to the nearest town. In the meantime, if it got dark before help arrived, we'd have to spend another night in the woods. The road was surprisingly free of traffic. Not a single vehicle had come by since we had pulled over.

The look of confusion on her face transitioned into betrayal. She looked at me as if I had planned my truck's breakdown here in a remote valley. I was not going to take her home after all. Who knew what I intended? Suddenly I felt tired. "Look," I said, "my truck is broken. I'm going to get it fixed, but if you stay with me you'll have to spend another night in the woods. You're welcome to stay, but you don't have to." I'm not sure what my eyes said. Maybe *You are safe with me, I'm not going to rape you.* Or maybe *Please leave, you are exhausting to be with.*

"How will I get to Hinton?" she asked me. Her tone was sharp. The answer seemed obvious to me. "The same way I will get to Alaska," I told her. "Just keep going in the right direction." She shouldered her pack and trudged slowly, dismally, along the highway until she disappeared over a ridge. I never saw her again. I worried, but I couldn't fix her life. Heck, I couldn't even fix my truck. I felt relief wash over me once she was gone. It is hard to be around someone who fears you. It was not a feeling I was used to. Perhaps I was not yet old enough to understand how hard it is to recover from certain kinds of damage.

As it turned out, had she stayed she would not have had to spend the night with her jackknife clenched in her fist. Just before sunset, a trucker stopped and helped me fashion a makeshift frost plug out of a piece of aspen. It was good enough to get me to the nearest town, where I would have gladly paid for her to stay in her own motel room—if only to get some relief from her persistent suspicion.

The next day I was on the road again. For me, going north was like going into purity. Alaska was a place I imagined myself living large and free. I could not understand why the girl was going back to the familiar ways of defeat. I see now that it was too easy for me to judge her. I saw her as resistant to my good faith, but perhaps her life had taught her that appearances are deceiving, and men—especially men who seem to care—are not to be trusted.

Since 1985 I've driven the long road to Alaska several times, but I've never stopped in Hinton. I think of it as the place from which the girl could not escape. It may very well be a nice town, but it exists for me as an archetype of despair that in the end gives way to numbness—which is, above all else, what I fear.

II. TEN YEARS AFTER I parted company with the girl from Hinton, I picked up another woman—this time, in a funky diner in Seattle, in a booth that was decorated like the inside of a cow's mouth. My intent this time was less innocent, but certainly not predatory. I was lonely. I wanted to spend the night with someone. The woman with whom I found myself in the bovine orifice struck me as sexy in a ragged, not-too-pretty sort of way. She didn't care that I earned my meager paycheck loading frozen chickens onto railroad cars. She looked like Janis Joplin, only older, and, of course, not dead. *This could be fun,* I thought.

We engaged in some first-date chat. She was a sculptor, she said. She liked to snowboard. She had a daughter from a previous marriage. When I asked her what her favorite movie was, she said *The Texas Chainsaw Massacre,* which I thought was a funny answer and a nice change from *Babette's Feast.* I thought she was kidding. She invited me to her trailer the next evening for dinner. I accepted the invitation. I was ready for a trailer park woman. She told me she made great chicken soup.

The first thing I noticed in her trailer was the zebra-striped curtains, of which I approved. The second thing I noticed was a provocative sculpture of a headless female torso, garishly painted and leaning forward as if traveling at great speed. The anatomy of the torso was freakishly exaggerated. The piece reminded me of a woman from a Robert Crumb cartoon—only liberated (perhaps by chainsaw?) of its head and legs. Despite the missing limbs, the voluptuous torso was disconcertingly and aggressively sexual. It seemed to be flying into a future in which no inhibitions would hinder it. It reminded me of the prow of a Viking warship. "Fly-ing Boobs and Butt," she said, in her barbed-wire voice. "That's the name of it."

For a while, things went pretty well. She had a quick wit and a punk-rock sensibility. She had lively music on the stereo—Mo-town, at my request. She gave me a beer, a hearty stout. She had good taste in beer. So far, so good. I tried to talk myself into believ-ing that there was nothing to be wary of.

But then she showed me pictures from the family album. One photo, in particular, caught my eye: she and her daughter, in a lighthearted mood, judging from the laughter, with their arms around each other's shoulders. The daughter was holding a pistol. The barrel of the gun was in her own mouth. I must have looked startled because my date quickly said, "Oh, we were just messing around. It wasn't loaded."

"Glad to hear it," I replied. It didn't seem like a very good choice for a mother-daughter bonding picture. I wondered who took the photo, and what sort of conversation might have accompanied the photo-op.

As I pondered these questions, she was telling me more about her daughter, and what a great relationship they had. By that point, I was only half-listening.

Knowing when to make an exit is sometimes a tricky busi-ness. I knew when I saw a picture of a teenage girl with a gun in her mouth—and mom with her arms around her, laughing—that I would not be spending the night in this trailer with the zebra-striped curtains and headless torso. Still, she had made dinner for me, and I felt that it would be rude to leave too abruptly. And per-haps I was overreacting. The picture, though creepy, did not prove anything. Did it? I would stay for the chicken soup.

When dinner came, the mood shifted without any warning to confessional. She had, as she put it, "family of origin issues." She wanted me to know that relationships were hard for her because she had been abused as a child. It felt a bit too soon—actually way too soon—for her to be talking about a relationship, or to be revealing intimate and painful details about her childhood. She, however, did not think it was too soon.

"My parents were very disturbed people," she continued. I studied my chicken soup, which was good, but not good enough to make me feel okay about the direction in which things were headed. But nothing could have prepared me for what came next. She had been raised, it turned out, by Satan worshippers who had forced her, as a toddler, to witness terrible things. Animal sacrifices. Human baby sacrifices.

I lifted my gaze from the soup and looked directly into her eyes—a gesture that she mistook as encouragement because she proceeded to provide details. I didn't feel like I was really there at her table, that maybe I was watching myself in a movie. I had a fleeting, unbidden thought: I don't know what is in this soup. After an awkward pause, I asked her if she remembered actually seeing these sacrifices.

She had shut them out of her psyche, she said, but a therapist had helped her recover the memories.

I shifted my gaze away from her and quickly took in the whole room: the curtains, the candles, the half-finished sculptures that now seemed like an assortment of bones. I suddenly wished the curtains were open so the streetlight could augment the glow of candles. In the prolonged silence, she leaned over and ladled another helping of soup into my bowl. It seemed like a way of holding me hostage. How does a person say no to homemade chicken soup?

In that moment, three possibilities entered my mind: These things really happened to her. These things didn't happen, but she thinks they did because someone helped her "recover" the memories. These things didn't happen and she knows it, but she wants me to think they happened. In all three cases, my response was the same: I want to get out of here.

Our eyes met again, and an unspoken dialogue took place in that meeting. This time she did not misinterpret my glance. It was the fulcrum of the evening. This is how it went: I looked up at her, and I'm pretty sure my eyes said, *Please, no more soup, because I am about to get out of here.* And her eyes said to me, *Oh shit, I've lost another one.*

To be honest, the next part of the story is kind of blurry. I don't remember what my words to her were at that point. Perhaps therapy would help me recover the memories. I think she asked me if I believed her, and I think my answer was "I don't know." I do remember that I didn't finish the soup. At the door, I thanked her for dinner and said I had to get some sleep because I worked the early shift at my job. On my way to the car, my momentum was similar to that of her statue, *Flying Boobs and Butt.*

III. AND HOW SHALL I end this? I want to tell a story with a different sort of ending, one in which strangers learn to see each other—if not with perfect understanding, then at least with some degree of trust, affection, and comprehension. My final vignette will be about Pearl, a woman with whom I exchanged helpless, inarticulate, frustrated glances. In the end, we found each other in the exchange.

I was working for an agency that offered recreational and physical therapy to clients with cerebral palsy and other disabilities. Pearl was one of my first clients, and her reputation preceded her. Some of the people who had previously worked with Pearl called her the Queen, and it was not clear whether this epithet was applied with affection or dread. Before my first scheduled outing with Pearl, my boss felt it necessary to prepare me. "Pearl can be ... how shall I say it ... well, a bit fussy and demanding. Aristocratic. She doesn't suffer fools." I wondered if my new boss already considered me a fool. "She is picky about her company, and she was very close to her last attendant. She may not welcome you. Good luck," she concluded grimly.

Our first outing was the Japanese Gardens in the Seattle Arboretum. Pearl loved botany, especially orchids, bonsai, and all manner of delicate and exotic plants. I arrived at Pearl's house at 1:35 p.m. Our outing was scheduled for 1:30, but since I had made the arrangements, I knew that we would have to wait at least twenty minutes for the ACCESS van to arrive. Pearl was waiting near the front door, in her wheelchair. She was dressed in a stylish white blouse and cape, and folded on her lap was a colorful afghan. A silk scarf was tied around her neck.

"Hello, Pearl," I said. I hoped that my greeting struck an appropriate balance between cheerfulness and dignity. "I'm pleased to meet you." She moved her head in what at first seemed like random fashion, until I saw that she was spelling out her response to me on the keyboard.

Pearl's severe cerebral palsy left her unable to speak, and she conversed in two ways. The more immediate way was through eye movement, but this method restricted her answers to yes or no. She would move her eyes up and to the right to answer yes, down and to the left if the answer was no. The more sophisticated way involved an electronic keyboard and voice box. Letters and common phrases were triggered by a light beam that came from a small device perched on the side of her head like an earpiece. Pearl had sufficient control of head movement to aim the light at the keyboard, and thus spell her messages.

Her first words to me, spoken in the metallic, bloodless, genderless voice of a machine: YOU ARE LATE.

The next few minutes were awkward. I don't remember what I said, but I remember that whatever it was, it was the wrong thing to say. Soon the van arrived. As we departed, Pearl's group home manager gave me a skeptical glance that I interpreted to mean *You're sure not going to last very long.* Once in the van, the driver secured Pearl's chair, and we were on our way to the garden. I spoke little during the ride. Since my seat was behind Pearl's, I couldn't tell if she cared one way or the other.

The Japanese Garden occupied about three or four acres of gently rolling terrain bisected by a creek. A pond sat in the center. Well-graded gravel paths braided through and around bamboo groves, sculptures, pagodas, shrines, boulders, and a plethora of flowering broadleaf evergreens and dwarf conifers. It was a magical place.

Pushing Pearl's chair was like pushing air. She was the lightest adult I had ever seen. The chair itself was a manual wheelchair of the simplest construction. (As I would later learn, Pearl thought motorized wheelchairs were "monstrosities." As she put it, she would rather sit still in a corner than terrorize the world.) It was easy to push her up the many hills.

I did not have any idea what kind of company she wanted, so I gave her, simply, myself. I talked when I felt like it, and lapsed into silence when I felt like it. I spoke of plants: I pointed out which pines held their needles in clusters of two, three, or five; which rhododendrons had fuzzy leaves, which ones had the most brilliant blossoms; the difference between clumping and running bamboo. I'm sure that in the course of the afternoon, I made several botanical puns and probably spouted some poetry.

After perhaps thirty minutes, I set the brake on her chair and offered my opinion about a rock garden. "The arrangement of stones is not right," I mused. "Too cluttered. It draws the eye to the left. The focus of attention should be here, where the brook enters the pond. The dance of light should be the first thing you see." This is what I said. What I thought was more like this: *She probably thinks I am a babbling idiot.* I looked over at her. YES, her eyes said. Was she responding to my comment, or could she read my mind? I would not have put it past her.

Still, as the outing went on, I became more comfortable with Pearl. After a while, it was time for another rest. We came to a bench by a weeping willow, and I set the brake on her chair and sat next to her. The late afternoon slant of sun caused small crescents to dance on the pond. I remember thinking that Pearl was not so difficult after all. It seemed to be going well.

And then it was not. I cannot say if this realization was gradual or sudden, because I don't know how long it felt to Pearl. My peripheral vision informed me that she was fidgeting in her chair, and when I looked directly at her, I knew something was wrong. I began to ask her questions: "Do you want to move on down the path?" NO. "Do you want to stay here?" NO. "Do you want to go home?" NO. "Are you in some sort of distress?" YES. "Can you tell me what the problem is?" NO.

I could see nothing amiss. She was sitting upright in her chair, the chair was on level ground with brakes engaged, her tray was level, her voice box and earpiece light were on. She was breathing okay, her afghan was in place. What was wrong?

"Is it a medical problem?" NO. "Do you need to be readjusted in your seat?" NO. "Do you need to use a restroom?" NO. "Do you need a drink of water?" NO. "Are you too cold or too hot?" NO. "Does the problem involve your chair?" NO. "Does it involve your body?" NO. "Does it involve your clothing?" NO. "Does it involve the weather?" NO. "Does it involve me?" NO.

No one else was in the garden that day. I wondered how it felt to be completely dependent on someone who could not figure out what you were trying to say.

"Are you in pain?" NO. "Are you worried about the time?" NO. "Do you want to stay here at the garden?" YES. "Do you want to move farther down the path?" NO. "Is the sun in your eyes?" NO. "Do you want something out of your bag?" NO. "Do you want me to call someone at your house?" NO.

I do not remember how many questions I asked, or how long we were there.

I began repeating questions I had already asked: "Do you need to be readjusted in your chair?" NO. "Do you need to use the restroom?" Pearl's vigorously impatient head-bobbing made the point that I had already asked these questions. This I understood clearly. "Am I missing something right under my nose?" I asked. YES YES YES.

In the telling of it, it all seems to go so quickly. But in the living of it, Pearl's distress and my inadequacy filled a lot of time and space. I simply could not figure out the problem. The game of twenty questions continued—only the number of questions far exceeded twenty.

"Listen, Pearl," I said, finally, trying to be calm. "I can't figure out what is wrong. I'm going to call for the ACCESS van, and I'm going to take you home." Pearl's eyes went down and to the left, over and over again: NO NO NO NO NO. "But I don't know what else to do," I protested. It seemed that her eyes said *keep trying.*

"Have any of my questions even come close to what is wrong?" NO. Finally I let a degree of exasperation show when I made a comment rather than asking a question. "I wish you would tell me using your board," I said.

Impatience filled her eyes as she moved her eyeballs frantically up and to the right: YES YES YES YES YES. And then, finally, a window opened up in my mind. "Pearl, I asked you earlier if you could tell me what was wrong, and you said no. Is there a problem with your communication board?" YES. "Are you able to use it?" NO. "Is the problem with your light?" NO YES. I didn't know what to make of this answer, so I moved on to another question. "Is the problem with your tray?" YES YES YES.

The problem was not immediately apparent. The board was level, the voice box engaged and functional, the light at her earpiece still on. But something was amiss. . . . Something looked odd. Suddenly I saw it. It was a subtle change in the position of the tray that held the keyboard. "The board is angled away from you," I said to Pearl. "The bumpy path has caused the board to wiggle, and now it is at an angle where your light can't trigger the keys. Am I right?" YES.

It only required a slight adjustment of the arm that held the keyboard, and a tightening of the wing nuts. It took about ten seconds to fix it. Pearl immediately got to work, aiming her light beam at the keys: F . . . I . . . N . . . A . . . L . . . L . . . Y. In case I was too dim of wit to follow her spelling, the mechanical voice rendered its unsentimental verdict: FINALLY. I knelt on the ground next to her and looked her in the eyes. "Pearl, I am a moron," I said. Her eyes agreed with that assessment. "Do you want to finish seeing the garden?" To my surprise, her eyes flashed YES. And so we finished the circuit around the bonsai trees. Then she let me know, with her board, what she wanted to see next. And next. And next.

As the ACCESS van was pulling into the parking lot, I asked one more question. "Do you want a different attendant next week?" NO.

Pearl's protector met us at the door with the same skeptical expression she had been wearing when we left. "Did you have a good outing?" She asked. In other words, did I pass the test? Her question was not directed at me. *Oh boy*, I thought. Here it comes. But without hesitation, Pearl's eyes moved up and to the right: YES. And that was the extent of her commentary. I wonder if she ever told anyone what really happened in the Japanese Garden.

I said good-bye to her, without any fuss, and was about to walk out the door. But Pearl's head was moving to and fro with great purpose. She had something to say. It took a while for her to spell it out: NEXT WEEK ARBORETUM BE ON TIME. When I arrived at precisely 1:29 on the following Thursday, she was waiting, wrapped in her trademark silk scarves. There was an unmistakable shine of good humor in her eyes.

I came to treasure my weekly outings with the Queen. They are the closest I shall ever come to living like royalty—although I was relegated to the role of butler. We became a pair about town, seen together at the museums, art galleries, botanical gardens, and tea rooms—she in her elegant scarves, me in my tattered Levi's jacket. "Should I dress up for our outings?" I once asked her. BE YOURSELF, the voice box said.

I got better at reading Pearl's moods as well as her eyes. We reached a point where I could predict her comments fairly accurately. We developed a kind of shorthand, a clipped vocabulary to minimize the use of her board. Much was said through eye contact alone—and the very slight movement at the corners of her mouth that indicated her dry humor and well-developed sense of irony. I don't know how, but I could often sense if she wanted me to just be quiet, or if she wanted to know, for instance, which plants I would prefer in a rock garden. She wanted to know my opinion about a variety of cultural questions: Did I prefer vases from the Ming Dynasty or the Han Dynasty? Mozart or Brahms? Which was my favorite Van Gogh? She might use a single word on her voice box: WHICH? WHY?

Although she did not eat or drink, she fully expected me, at an artist's reception, to sample the cookies and take a spot of tea, and to entertain her with droll comments about the exhibition. In many ways, she lived a full life of the senses, vicariously, through my observations. I came to understand that although Pearl was a woman of great dignity, she knew how to laugh at the indignities of life that affected her. She liked to share private jokes.

One of the outings I most enjoyed was to the greenhouses on Capitol Hill. Her chair was narrow enough, and her body light enough, that I could navigate down any aisle. On a blustery winter day, the steamy greenhouses were our refuge. I would hold blossoms to her nose, or gently trace leaves along her cheek so that she could feel the various textures of the foliage. I would speak to her the botanical and common names of whatever we passed, and I have no doubt that she held many of those names in her memory.

I have not seen Pearl for many years. Much older than me and in poor health to begin with, she has surely passed away by now. I hope that her ashes are in a garden somewhere.

ON THE ROAD TO GRAND FALLS

SOMETIMES, WHEN I'M tired of all the shit, I just want to close my eyes and imagine I'm in my old turquoise '66 Chevy pickup, going way too fast, with two tires on the high track and two on the low, leaning tipsily close to disaster, and leaving a trail of dust in my wake on the road to Grand Falls. It's easy to feel myself once again fishtailing through cinders, spinning donuts and brodies on a playa of sticky red mud. It makes me smile.

By "all the shit," I mean the pressure I put on myself, the daily worries and anxieties, the slow buildup of disappointments that gradually gum up the workings of my soul the way plaque adheres to the walls of aging arteries. I get weary of trying to understand what I should have done, or still should do, with my life. Doubts assail me, especially doubts about myself. Am I useful in the world? Do I make a difference? I don't know. But today I say . . . fuck usefulness. I don't want to be useful. I just want to be back on that road, driving headlong into open country.

So start with space and silence and a road that pulls you in. Add wind and an aching blue sky. Elegant sweeping curves of black cinder hills contrasting with the long straight lines of the Painted Desert, the blocky geometry of sandstone. It's a stark landscape, with few hiding places. People who have grown up in cities or in lush and fertile places can feel naked and exposed out here. Not everyone likes it. But I remember the words of a Navajo kid who went back east to study at a college in Michigan. He dropped out and came back home after one semester. Claustrophobia got to him. "I needed to stretch my eyes," he said.

Nakedness isn't such a bad metaphor. If trees are like the land's clothes, then a drive from Flagstaff to Grand Falls is a striptease. The high mountains are thickly dressed in blue spruce and groves of quaking aspen. As the slopes taper off, open, parklike forests of ponderosa pine dominate. The handsome ponderosas thin out into sparser piñon pines, which in turn give way to gnarled Utah juniper. The junipers stake claim to little pockets and isolated ridgelines, like Navajos who don't want to build their hogans within sight of a neighbor. The scattered junipers dwindle into wind-shaven cheatgrass, and by the time you get to the falls, you are down to the red skin of the earth.

///

If there is any landscape that has shaped my identity, it is the cinder hill country northeast of Flagstaff and the high desert around Grand Falls. There are many craters: Merriam, Sheba, Black Bottom, Strawberry, and SP are among my favorites. Beyond the craters, the Little Colorado River wanders across the Painted Desert. The river is often dry, sometimes a trickle, and in periods of high snowmelt or after heavy monsoon thunderstorms, a torrent of muddy water.

I don't think there was any place during my adolescence that I went to more often. I must have gone out there about once a week, for a couple of years. I learned to be myself there, sometimes in the presence of others, but usually alone. At midnight, in January, under a full moon, I'd fill a thermos with hot coffee and climb Merriam Crater. Or on a hot July day with a cold bottle of beer. Or at five in the morning, to catch the sunrise.

One thing I liked to do was run. Park the truck anywhere and go. The route was always spontaneous and different, but it usually circumnavigated one of the bigger craters or a cluster of the smaller ones. Sometimes I followed the rim above the Little Colorado River. After running I would find a place to watch the sunset. I liked to stay out long enough to see the sky transition to stars. In the high desert, stars are scattered across the sky like sand in a sand painting. If I was in an area that had any trees, I'd search for some dead wood and make a fire. The pitchy pine and redolent, sweet-smelling juniper burned with hungry, crackling intensity. It is perhaps the best smell on earth.

Once I climbed Merriam Crater on New Year's Day, when my head was as gnarled as the oak rounds on my back porch that needed splitting. I had had too much to drink the night before and harbored no resolutions worth keeping. The new year filled me with dread. So I drove the Chevy to the base of the crater and began to climb up the shifting cinders. I startled some antelope and watched them bound over bunches of Mormon tea. I put one foot in front of the other in a mindless cadence until, breathing hard and sweating, I stood at the crater's rim. On the summit, I lay down and took a nap. Old year, new year . . . it didn't matter. I was at the center of the world and the center of myself, and I could stay there indefinitely. I made only one resolution that year: to remember how that place gave itself to me, and to accept the gift graciously.

Many people hang-glide and paraglide off the summit of Merriam. The conditions are ideal: a steep but uniformly smooth slope, wide open country all around, sunny days all year, and a persistent wind sweeping upslope from the desert. I did this only once, not from the summit, but from a knoll about halfway up the crater on its north side. I will never forget the incredible feeling of being lifted and welcomed into the sky.

Imagine running down the slope of Merriam Crater with a glider and feeling the stiff upslope wind effortlessly lift you. Soar, then, above the wide sweep of cinder hills, catching thermals, wheeling slowly like a red-tailed hawk above the Painted Desert. What do you see? To the west, the snowcapped San Francisco Peaks, holy mountains, home of the kachina spirits. To the south, the wintergreen swell of the Mogollon Rim, like a weir over which the land-scape flows into the rough-and-tumble backwash of the Mazatzal and Sierra Ancha Mountains. To the east, the Hopi Buttes, hard-ened plugs of ancient volcanoes, standing guard over the three me-sas the Hopis consider the center of the world. To the north, the Little Colorado weaves its rusty way past bluffs of sandstone fluted by erosion. Directly underneath, the beloved cinder hills.

Just over those low hills to the left is Strawberry Crater and its jagged lava flow sprawling, as the Navajo say, like the dried blood of a giant. That speck beyond it is Hank's Trading Post. The long ridge is the Echo Cliffs, with Tuba Butte at the end. Roden Crater and Grand Falls down there. Right below is the Sproul—concen-tric half circles of basalt ridges, like the rings of an onion cut in two. To the right is Canyon Diablo, the Devil's Canyon. I used to climb there, looking for eagles' nests. It winds past Two Guns, which is nothing more than the burnt-out husk of a service station. A SHELL sign, missing the *S*, rises above the ruins. Or at least it used to, in the memories of my teenage years.

Most of the time, I went out to the craters and the falls alone. That was part of the point—to get away from people. But I do have some great memories of being there with others: sometimes friends, sometimes family, and once in a while with complete strangers. I once spent a day in the craters with a girl from New York City. I don't even remember how it happened; some odd set of circum-stances brought us together. The only thing I knew about her was her name.

When we started out in the morning, she talked incessantly. Mostly she described parties, acid trips gone wrong, and various dissolute musicians she associated with. But no one can talk all day, and when it was my turn I gave her botany lessons: this is rabbit-brush, this is four-winged saltbush, this is Mormon tea. As the day evolved, it became evident to her that I wasn't angling for sex, and I didn't have any drugs in my truck. I was a Christian, I told her, and a day with me was likely to be boring. The pace of the conversation slowed, but it seemed not to be due to boredom. We opened up to each other slowly, patiently. Periods of silence became more common as she began to realize that she liked the sound of the wind. As dusk approached, I took her back to the place where she was staying in Flagstaff. It had been a nice day with her. I never heard from her again.

The dirt road to Grand Falls branched off of a paved road that went to the small reservation town of Leupp. For a road with little traffic, there were plenty of hitchhikers, and I often picked them up. Almost always they were Navajos or Hopis on their way back to the reservation after a weekend in Flagstaff. The narrative usually involved some relative who had brought them into town on Friday and somehow lost track of them by Sunday.

On one occasion, I picked up a young Hopi man outside of Mary's Café, which was the last chance a hungry person had to snag some greasy hash browns before leaving town. I was in college at the time, and he seemed to be about the same age. As soon as he sat down in the passenger seat, I recognized him as someone I knew from high school. We hadn't been friends exactly, but we had shared an art class and I had often wandered by his table in that class to see what he was doing. I admired his talent.

He recognized me too, and as often happens, we were soon playing the did-you-know-so-and-so game. We had inhabited different social circles, but in a small high school there is bound to be some overlap. He mentioned the name of a Navajo kid. "Oh yes," I replied. "He punched me in the face one time." He offered up the name of another. "I knew him. He beat me up too." After a moment of silence, he said, "Yeah, I didn't get along with Indians either."

I dropped him off in Leupp. "See you around," I said, but I never did see him again. I heard later that he had joined the Marines. He was a truly gifted artist who had paintings in several Flagstaff galleries, and I hope he kept on painting. I vividly remember a charcoal sketch he made in that high school art class: the adobe homes of a Hopi pueblo, gently cradled in a giant pair of ancient, wrinkled hands. The sketch was titled *The Old Ones*.

I treasure the memory of a time that I went to Grand Falls with one of my best friends. It was an unexpected trip; he showed up at my house on a Saturday, and off we went. We took the Chevy up Sheba Crater but had to turn around just shy of the top. The loyal truck growled and bucked and ripped through cinders, but it just couldn't do it. I don't know how much rubber I burned off of my tires. So we gave up and headed down the road to Grand Falls. As always, the country opened up to some elemental desire to go fast, and so we did.

When we reached the falls, we found it swollen with spring runoff. Water filled the channel from side to side. We hiked to the bottom, through sticky muck that sucked at our shoes, and then up to the broad shelf that separates the upper falls from the lower. Along the shelf, on the left side of the falls, there is a house-sized boulder. A large part of the river's flow plunges onto this boulder and is cleaved by the prow of this rock into torrential twin streams. It is possible (or at least used to be) to actually get behind the boulder into an undercut pocket of the sandstone cliff and look out through the curtain of thundering chocolate water.

This memory is important to me because over the course of a few years, I had gradually grown apart from this friend. We had been close in middle school, but in high school we found ourselves out of sync. It was my fault. Having become an Evangelical Christian, I had fallen into the trap of trying to convert my friend to a view of the world that he didn't naturally hold. I think I became kind of annoying. As a result, our times together were not as free and easy as they had been before. We didn't often do things together anymore—just for the simple joy of adventure, laughter, and good company. But on that day, on the road to Grand Falls, I felt restored to the friendship we once had. No posturing, no persuading, no talk of what one ought to believe.

What I'm talking about is loving the world, and sometimes I forget to do that. Sometimes I'm so concerned with the future of the world that I forget the pleasure of just being in the world. In the past week, I have been trying to write a good, articulate essay about politics and what we call the "environment" (I hate that term), but the words just weren't flowing. I've been trying to understand how I feel about so many recent events: Occupy Wall Street, the polarization of society, the many ways in which we seem to be unraveling. In the midst of my work, I just got sick of it.

In high school, as a born-again Christian, I thought I had all the answers. Now I'm a middle-aged, balding hippie. My views have changed a lot. Maybe I still think I have the answers. I probably come across that way, even though I don't mean to. I talk to my friends about things like politics and farming and climate change and species extinctions because I don't think we have much time to get things right. It seems to me that we have seriously damaged the world, and I'm worried about the future. Are my opinions correct? Well I don't know. They are my opinions. I would be happy, actually, to have time prove me wrong. I don't really want to be right about some of these things.

Anyway, I don't like always talking and writing about problems. It makes me grumpy. I don't like how it can erode friendships. Some of my very favorite people in the world don't share my political, social, or ecological convictions. Rather than arguing, I would like to be with some of those people at Grand Falls, drinking beer and laughing, telling stories, having a good time. Yes, I've got convictions just like everyone else, and despite the tone of this essay, I'll still have them tomorrow. But today I want something else. Freedom and sunshine in open country. I want to feel happy and reckless and perfectly at home in a natural playground that will never change.

So when I got tired of the essay I was trying to write, I took a break and listened to some of my favorite music. That's when it happened. I played two songs by the Native American jazz musician Jim Pepper. The songs spoke to me, as songs do, at a level deeper than words.

And that's when I knew that I was going to write about the road to Grand Falls.

The first song perfectly captured the feeling of racing headlong into open space, soaring off the edge of a crater, or taking a long run in the clean light of an October day through the cinder hills. The second song brought me down peacefully beside a fire pit near the river, at that moment just before the sun slips away and the chocolate brown flow of the Little Colorado River turns to burnished gold. I was there, again, wrapping a rainbow trout in foil, with some butter and lemon and onion, and placing it in the hot coals. Then eating it with my fingers, as the last light of the sun tinges the mare's tails in the sky the same color as the flesh of the trout. Waiting for the stars to come out.

Jim Pepper's saxophone lifts my spirit, just as an updraft on Merriam Crater might lift a hang glider. His music flows like water in the desert. His songs fill me with clean, simple, animal happiness. His songs remind me that I am equal parts body and spirit, forever intertwined and connected to the dust and wind and water. The songs, "Witchi Tai To" and "Comin' and Goin'," are from the splendid album *Comin' and Goin'*. These are old favorites; I listen to them whenever I need to feel peaceful and free.

While I was listening to the music, I searched through my old photographs. I didn't turn up much. For all the times I went out to Grand Falls, I only have one or two good pictures. I never took a camera in those days. Maybe photography is the art of people old enough to understand mortality. I probably thought I would always be able to go there. So I looked up the falls up on YouTube—everything these days is on YouTube—and found a pretty good video of the river in flood, which flooded me with memories and emotions. A person is similar to a river channel: sometimes empty, sometimes trickling, sometimes all the force of life coming down at once.

If you've ever been to Grand Falls, if you've ever gone barreling down that road, if you've ever felt like you could turn into wind and just keep going, then try this: If you can find them, listen to these songs by Jim Pepper, close your eyes and let the music put you back into that windswept country. For that matter, give it a try even if you haven't been to the falls. Let Pepper's sax bless you and keep you, let the Arizona sun shine upon you and give you peace. Let the music take you to the falls, to the unexpected and abundant grace of water in the desert.

In those simple days, on the road to Grand Falls, I didn't think too much. I just drove fast, sang loud, ran hard, got wet, stripped down to my shorts, and basked in the warm sun. I liked to go when the spring runoff from the White Mountains was a sign that winter was releasing its grip, and soon the juice of new life would be evident everywhere. The sun on my skin made me feel happy, horny, and healthy. Now, I'm on the brink of turning fifty, and it's kind of embarrassing to use the word *horny* in an essay. What happened? Did I just get old?

"It's good where we've been and where we're going," Pepper sings. It's hard to feel cynical or depressed when he sings it. The state of the world is not how I would have it, but it is still a beautiful world. And it's the only one we have. Job number one: just be. Be filled, like a river fed by snowmelt. Be lifted up and carried away. Be a human being, at home in the world. Be glad to be alive.

Amen. That's how I want to feel every day of my life. I want to feel like the wind. Like that water, crashing down. Like that boy I once was, crazy with light and speed, fishtailing through cinders, spinning donuts with his '66 Chevy in the greasy mudflats.

CROSSING THE DISTANCE

A LONG-DEAD GREEK fellow by the name of Zeno told the tale of a race between Achilles and a tortoise. If you will recall, Achilles gave the tortoise a head start. After all, how hard can it be to pass a tortoise? To his dismay, Achilles discovered that he couldn't catch up, because, of course, it's impossible to cross an infinite distance. No matter the size of the gap, it can always be cut in half, over and over. No matter how much distance is covered, more remains. Movement, Zeno would have us believe, is an illusion. Think you are getting somewhere? Think again.

Ah, those Greeks! We also have them to thank for the stories of Sisyphus, whose fate it was to roll a boulder up a hill for all eternity, and of Tantalus, who could never quite reach the tempting cluster of grapes just above his head. And the Greeks didn't corner the market on this cheery theme: a few centuries later, on the ceiling of the Sistine Chapel, Michelangelo painted God and Adam trying to reach out and touch each other. The gap between their fingers is the centerpiece of the painting. (It occurs to me that all these examples are of men. Do women know how to get somewhere?)

Maybe Zeno's paradox is a trick. After all, I move every day. I cross distances and reach destinations. Don't I? Well, I don't know if movement is an illusion or not, but sometimes I feel like Achilles trying to catch the tortoise. Every New Year's Eve, the same resolutions pop up in my head as if they were fresh ideas. My student loans never seem to shrink. I lose my keys over and over again. (Or have I only lost them once, in the eternal now?) At any rate, questions remain: How should I measure change? How can I speak of growth? How can I ever cross the finish line, go the distance, reach the destination?

The stimulus for these ruminations was a seven-hour drive home after a miserable performance in a track meet a few weeks ago. I drove home with a bronze medal, but since there were only three runners in my race, this did not console me. For six months, I had been trying to improve my time in the 400 meters, and I had high hopes for doing so at the Canadian Masters National Indoor Championships. Alas, after running my race, I understood the stories of both Achilles and of Sisyphus.

I'd brought a book to read in the motel the night before the meet, *Chaos: Making a New Science* by James Gleick. Neither chaos theory nor the book (published in 1987) is new anymore. But it was new to me. If my goal was to read something that might help me finish a race in better time, choosing Gleick was a mistake. As if Zeno's famous race wasn't discouraging enough, Gleick introduced me to a mathematical perversity known as the Koch snowflake.

The Koch snowflake is an ever-expanding shape enclosed within a finite perimeter. Start with two intersecting equilateral triangles: a Star of David. This is the basic template for the snowflake. The points of the star make six smaller equilateral triangles. Now, make the middle third of each side of these six triangles the base of another, smaller triangle that juts outward. This results in a Star of David with cute little prickles on it. Repeat this step again, again, and again. . . . Each addition lengthens the snowflake's perimeter by one-third. Soon you will need a microscopic pencil. You can increase the perimeter forever—if you have forever at your disposal. At some point in the project, simply draw a circle around the snowflake, and there you have it: an infinitely expanding shape, contained within the circle.

The snowflake flirts with the concept of boundlessness within limits. How can such a thing be? I am a mathematical idiot, perhaps too easily impressed. Geometry is as far as I got in high school—and I barely squeaked through that. No doubt some people I know could explain, in between yawns, how these things can in fact be. But even I am clever enough to see that the perimeter of a Koch snowflake is *potentially,* rather than *actually,* infinite. Its infinity can only be realized in eternity. It's not infinite in the meantime. In other words, don't pay an architect to draw you one. (At least don't pay by the hour.) It is, one might say, a conceptual reality, rather than an embodied one. An embodied reality . . . well, has a body.

I like bodies. That's why I run. At least it is partly why I run. I understand bodies better than I do conceptual snowflakes. When the contemplation of infinity and eternity makes me dizzy, I retreat into the life of the body. It's where I'm most comfortable. That's why, whenever I am confused, I go to the track. It doesn't relieve my confusion, but it usually makes me feel better. Lately, however, I've been seeing evidence of infinity even within the body and its very evident limits.

My favorite pastime, sprinting, exhibits a Sisyphean pointlessness that might appeal to the sort of mathematician who enjoys a Koch snowflake. Consider, for instance, the 400-meter dash: What could be more pointless than running around in a circle? The 400 is a perfect exercise in both futility and masochism: the point is to end up exactly where you started, but in as much pain as possible. What could be more fun than that?

A 400-meter track is a circle squashed into an oval. A somewhat flattened Koch snowflake might fit within it, where the football field is. In the final 100 meters of the 400, it's easy to believe that infinity can be surreptitiously folded within the circle. When the body is awash with lactic acid, it's easy to believe, with Zeno, that movement is an illusion. It's also easy to believe that time is elastic, and not all minutes are of equal duration. But, miraculously, I do in fact cross the distance to reach something called a finish line, and it seems real enough. It happens in less than a minute.

How can eternity be condensed into a minute? Or, to put it another way: How can a minute expand enough to hold eternity? I suspect, when I consider the questions I've just asked, that I'm not framing the inquiry correctly in the first place. My real concern is a different sort of journey, one that crosses neither time nor meters, but rather some sort of distance more difficult to measure. I may not be smart enough to know what to call it—much less how to measure it—so it stands to reason that I don't know if I've crossed it. But there have been a few situations in my life where I felt outside of time, situations that seemed both to last forever and to take no time at all. These situations are hard to describe. I don't even know what verb tense to use.

Many years ago—if I may be permitted to assume chronology—I attended seminary, where I struggled with verbs. To be precise, I struggled with verbs of the future perfect tense in the Greek New Testament. I won't try very hard to explain the future perfect tense as used in the New Testament, except to say that it means something like *already . . . and not yet,* as in Saint Paul's dubious assurance to believers that "You have been (already and not yet) sanctified." Perhaps Paul was acquainted with Zeno.

I expressed my confusion to my Greek professor, who said, reassuringly, "Our sanctification is a done deal. It just isn't done yet." That made it clear as mud. His explanation seemed to strain the meaning of the word *done,* but he was smarter than me, so I assumed he knew what he meant. Sensing that my grasp of the future perfect tense was tenuous, he elaborated. "It is prophetic. This verb tense refers to something that has already been accomplished but the effects of which have not yet been realized." I looked at him blankly, and then said, "So, in the meantime. . . ."

It's a common phrase: In the meantime. What is this thing called *the meantime*? My Greek professor might have described it as the part of the prophetic future perfect tense captured by the words *not yet.* I think of it as a gap. Think of the gap between Achilles and the tortoise, between Tantalus and his grapes, and, in Michelangelo's painting, between Adam and God. The meantime is the moment in which Sisyphus sighs, rolls up his sleeves, and says "Oh, well." The Buddha might say it is the moment in which desire exists—and, of course, is not fulfilled. It's the distance between what is, and what is next. Can you cross it?

I was driven to seminary by a kind of thirst. I can't get more precise than that. In hindsight I'm not sure that I understood it. I don't understand it now. Some people may nod their heads earnestly and say, "You were searching for God." Maybe. I don't know if most of us know what we mean by such statements. At any rate, my time in seminary was not as memorable as the journey that brought me there, in the summer of 1986.

On my way to seminary, I crossed the states of Virginia and West Virginia on a bicycle. My goal was not to overtake a tortoise, but to cross the Ohio River—my version of the river Jordan—and meet up on the other side with my friend Matt. Matt was a gregarious fellow, an unlikely combination of Puerto Rican blood, a backwoods Georgia upbringing, and Dutch Calvinist theology. He was a Holy Ghost Warrior in a black pickup truck. We were both on our way to Michigan, where we had enrolled in seminary to become (after mastering those troublesome verbs) preachers. We both believed in the possibility of change, of redemption, of forward progress, of winning the race set before us.

I believed, also, in traveling light, so for my bike trip I just threw some clothes and a sleeping bag in a duffel bag and called it good. Taking my cue from San Juan de la Cruz, the fourteenth-century Spanish mystic who wandered barefoot across Spain making shoes for the poor, I had decided to keep my preparations to a minimum and to move with boldness into the future God had planned for me, unhindered by possessions, worry, or common sense.

So I had no helmet, no headlight, no spare tubes, no tent, no credit card, no spandex tights, and no bicycle pump. (I vacillated in regard to the pump, understanding its almost certain utility, but determined that I had just enough money in my wallet for food. I would have to trust God to provide adequate tire pressure.) What else did I have? Zeal, of course. A surplus of youthful energy, a tattered copy of *Dark Night of the Soul*, and a hammer. At least I didn't follow the example of Juan de la Cruz in every respect. I wore shoes.

I had started my journey in Fairbanks, Alaska. I didn't have my own car, having relieved myself of that particular burden before leaving the north. My friend Peggy graciously let me drive her

Honda from Fairbanks to Arizona, and then to Norfolk, Virginia, where I dropped it off for her at her new home. All across the country, I slept outside wherever I felt like throwing my bag. I met all kinds of interesting people. But I needed to find my own way across the Appalachians, so I got the cheapest Huffy bicycle Kmart could provide and was soon on my way.

I had five days to reach Ohio, where I would meet Matt, who was driving his pickup from Georgia. Aside from that, my only plan was to not have a plan—and I followed that plan exactly. My timing for this trip coincided with a hurricane that delivered a glancing blow to the Virginia coast. I couldn't wait for the weather to change, so Peggy drove me to Richmond, where the wind was a bit less extreme than in Norfolk. I parted ways with my friend in the middle of the night, during a torrential downpour. She may have thought I was unhinged.

Not more than twenty miles out of Richmond, on an obscure country road, I suffered my first breakdown: without warning or apparent cause, one of my foot pedals simply fell off. Just like that. In the horizontal rain and fierce wind, without a flashlight or headlamp, I fixed it the only way available to me: by beating on it with my hammer. (If you ask me why I carried a hammer, I will tell you that I took it just in case a foot pedal fell off.) After banging the petal back onto the sprocket, I remounted the Huffy and rode for fifteen hours straight. There was no point in trying to sleep, since everything in my duffel was soaked, and there was no patch of ground that had not been rendered a bog.

On day two, the sun came out. "Jesus rays" pierced the clouds, and I crossed Shenandoah bathed in splendid golden light. My butt hurt like hell, but it didn't diminish my enthusiasm. The corrugated land rippled away in all directions, its contours softened by dense flora and fuzzy air. I reveled in the eastern trees, the tight weave of dogwood and alder, and the mitten hands of sassafras. On day three, I entered West Virginia. If a line is the shortest distance between two points, then there are no lines in West Virginia. Neither are there any flat spots. Biking this country was hard work. Steep, narrow roads with no shoulder wound ceaselessly up hills, down into hollows, and over again. At the bottom of each hollow, a small creek babbled like a Holy Roller speaking in tongues.

When evening came, I spread my bag under the jagged crags of Seneca Rocks. On the morning of day four, the first rays of the sun split into a rainbow by dew that gathered itself on the downy underside of tall grasses. Before leaving Seneca Rocks, I climbed ropeless as far as I dared up the beautiful sandstone and watched a hawk circling. Late in the day, near Elkins, I met a soft-spoken botanist with a prodigious beard who walked me through the forest on his homestead and taught me the eastern trees. It turned out that what seemed a mature forest to my western eyes was actually second growth over hills scarred by a century of coal mining and bad farming, an impoverished landscape sparse in both wildlife and plant diversity. Like all of us, damaged but beautiful anyway. The botanist offered me a dry bed for the night, and his gracious wife cooked a meal of corned beef, cabbage, and potatoes while she soothed my ears with her lovely Dutch accent.

On the fifth day, I veered away from my path, drawn northward to the town of Fairmont, where there was to be a revival meeting that very night. All over West Virginia, I had been seeing posters announcing a night of worship and exhortation, with maybe some healing and prophesy thrown in for good measure. Leading it all was a man who was famous in evangelical circles for ministering to gangsters and drug addicts in one of the roughest neighborhoods of New York City. He was a man I admired—I thought.

A preacher in training should hear a preacher, so I rode hard into Fairmont. I was wound up with excitement. The revival was being held in a football stadium, and it was well underway when I arrived. It looked like a couple of thousand people were in attendance. A low hum emanated from the crowd, like the hum of power lines. As I entered the stadium, the hum differentiated into individual voices, speaking in the cadences peculiar to Pentecostal Christians unleashed. The hum quieted, but the sense of zealous anticipation did not diminish when the evangelist began to speak.

That night, more than anything else, I wanted to believe in the transformative power of grace. I wanted, as a matter of fact, to be transformed by such grace. I wanted the Holy Spirit to move through me as a wave moves through water and the wind moves through trees. I wanted to be inspired—which means, literally, to be filled with breath. I wanted the breath of God to move through me. But the night would not unfold as I had expected. I would in fact be inspired by the revival, but in a funny ass-backward sort of way.

The famous evangelist had a lot to say, but he spoke more of sin than of grace. He seemed to be on intimate terms with a God who was going to throw many people into a lake of fire. His righteous ire was particularly aimed at homosexuals and secular humanists, emphasizing not only their willful depravity, but also their intent to deceive the weak of mind and tempt the weak of will. It was 1986, and AIDS was ravaging the gay community in many American cities, and the evangelist said the disease was God's righteous judgment on Sodomites. He went on to condemn the secular humanists that had wrested control of the universities and the public schools and were poisoning the nation's youth. He heaped contempt on the liberal Christians who were letting it all happen. They were, he insisted, not really Christians at all.

As he preached, I thought of my siblings who were dedicated teachers. I considered my father, a university math professor, a gentle, humble man and a liberal Christian. I recalled my dear friend Peggy, a humanist who had taught me to love poetry and to keep my eyes open for the beauty in the world—whether or not it could be explained by my theology. I thought of friends I knew, people of integrity who experienced no shame in loving partners of their own gender.

I had gone to the revival seeking a night of love and praise. What I found instead was self-righteousness and—there is no other word for it—malice. My pulse quickened as I considered what I had always heard and believed about this man. I realized I had been mistaken. Neither the tone nor the substance of the evangelist's message fit my expectation. I couldn't see into the man's soul; I could only tell that I didn't trust him. He claimed to be guided by grace, but I discerned no grace in his words.

All day long I had wanted to attend the revival; it was as if my pedaling feet had been guided to this destination. But now, in an instant, I knew that I needed to get out. This need was too visceral to be called a choice. It was more like a need to breathe—which is, literally, a need to be inspired.

It took some physical effort to leave. It was like leaving a rock concert. I was in the front of the large crowd and had to aggressively shoulder my way past worshippers with their hands raised. On my way out, my eyes briefly connected with the eyes of a woman. We exchanged no words but her glance seemed to ask me "What's the matter, don't you want to praise the Lord?" I'm sure my eyes gave the unequivocal answer, "not yours."

Sometimes confusion propels the journeys we must take. I had planned to sleep somewhere near Fairmont, but I knew now that I would not be able to sleep. I straddled my bike and began to pedal with a ferocity born of cognitive dissonance. The revival had left me wondering who I was, what I believed, and who "my people" were. Picturing the man whose testimony I had just heard, I thought to myself *Lord, whoever I am on my way to becoming, let it not be that*.

That night in West Virginia is a sharp-edged memory. The August air was muggy and thick. The road was blessedly empty of traffic, and I weaved crazily from side to side. Wind whipped through my hair. Lightning shredded the horizon. Oblivious to time and fatigue, I moved through the landscape as a gathering wave moves through water. I didn't tire. Or perhaps it's more accurate to say that I did tire, but I pushed through it. I found more breath than I had ever found before. Many centuries ago, Saint Benedict said "work is prayer," and that night I poured my spirit into a prayer expressed not in words, but in work. I prayed with quads, glutes, hamstrings, and breath. I prayed with lactic acid.

Surely I was moving—but toward what? Toward peace and joy, I hoped. Toward a certainty of things unseen, I hoped. Most of all, I hoped to be moving toward grace and freedom. It took some time, but at some point in the night, I quit thinking and began to feel free. A verse of Scripture rose to the surface of my awareness and lingered till dawn: "My yoke is easy and my burden is light." For a few blessed hours, anyway, it was true. I didn't trouble myself with questions; the bad taste of the revival faded and was replaced by the simple sensation of speed, the smells of a summer night, and the fickle glow of fireflies in thickets along the road. There was no need to prove anything, understand anything, protest anything.

Such moments are fleeting, as we all know. They are like faint stars that vanish when you look at them directly. Yet in another way they stay with you forever. I am tempted to say that the night didn't pass at all—that I am still in it. But of course, in the usual way that we measure change, which is to say, *in time,* it did pass. At sunrise, I arrived at the banks of the Ohio River, with its old, metallic surface, its inscrutable currents. I would cross that river into a new life, and I hoped that in that new life, the twin stars of grace and freedom would not be elusive.

Alas, they did prove elusive. I met some truly good people at seminary, but increasingly I did not feel at home among them. After a year of banging my head against the sacred walls, I realized that I had not found my place after all, and it was time to get out once again. Sometimes we are moving but not toward the destination we assume. I thought I was headed toward deeper assurance and certainty in my faith when actually I was moving away from it. As it turned out, the Ohio River was not my Jordan, and Michigan was not my Promised Land.

I had a small taste of freedom on that August night in West Virginia. It was tentative—like a star too faint to be seen directly, like a flickering firefly—yet it also seemed more eternal and more enduring than the usual goals and obligations and mistakes that we can put on a list. What is freedom, and how do we get there? That is a complicated question. For me, part of the answer lies in trusting my own inclinations, even when they go against what I think I should believe. It is, I suppose, letting go of what burdens me. Sometimes it takes a long time to do that. Accurate diagnosis of one's burdens is long-term work.

From what burdens would I like to be set free? Here is a partial list: I would like to be free from the incessant yammering of salesmen, the manipulations of politicians, the claptrap of church, the straightjackets of doctrine. I would like to be free from the should-haves and the could-haves that clutter my mind late at night. I would like to be free of resentments that poison the well of joy. I would like to be free from the traps of self-pity, self-doubt, and self-consciousness.

I would like to enter into the freedom that comes from losing the self. I would like to be fully present in each moment, fully engaged with each person who comes my way, and so be freed from regrets about the past and worries about the future. I would like to be free to grow old gracefully, without bitterness. I would like to be free of the need to be right, or the need to be certain. I would like to be free of the desire to judge others, so that I might hear and attend to them instead.

I'd like to be free of debt. For that matter, I'd like to be free of money altogether. I'd like to be free of both the fear of failure and the need for success. I'd like to be free of the insistent desire to own things. I'd like to be free of the desire to control others, or to elevate myself at their expense. I'd like to be free of the desire to hurt others or make them feel small. I'd like to be free of the constant noise that follows me around daily so I can hear my inner voice and find my center and make my own decisions.

I know of a woman who for thirty-five years was married to a man who sought to control every detail of his environment. (He considered his wife part of his environment.) I won't go into the sorry details of their marriage. Suffice it to say that she was trapped. She thought it was an arrangement ordained by God. Movement, for so many years, did not seem possible to her.

One day she decided to leave. Just like that. When she left her husband, the only thing of his that she took were his neckties. (I should explain. This man had a dresser in which each drawer contained socks of a different color. In his basement, he had stockpiled enough toilet paper to last a century. In his walk-in closet there was a wraparound tie rack that held hundreds of meticulously arranged neckties.)

She drove away from what had been her existence, with her husband's ties in a disheveled pile in the passenger seat. I can imagine her accelerating down the interstate, rolling down the window, feeling the wind on her face. This is how I see it: She drives with one hand. With the other, she reaches into the pile of ties, and one by one, releases them out the open window. She sees them in the rear-view mirror, flapping wildly, then fluttering without fuss to the pavement, like butterflies alighting on blossoms. Her movement toward freedom is measured by the periodic appearance of neckties on the highway.

How do we move into freedom? I'm not sure I can answer that, for me or for anyone else. I'm still working on it. I think we all have to find our own way, and we have to do it over and over again. Sometimes we make mistakes; or at least I do. Just as on that bike trip across West Virginia, I sometimes think I am moving toward a goal, when in fact I am moving away from it. Some of my biggest mistakes involve contradictions that seem obvious—in hindsight. If I experience God as an ineffable mystery, for instance, then why go to a school where the intent is to explain the mystery?

And, more recently, there is this one: If my goal is to embrace simplicity, then why take out huge student loans to enroll in a ridiculously expensive university? I hoped to learn how to pursue ecological and economic sustainability, social justice, and self-sufficiency in both my own life and in society. What was I thinking? It's like shelling out big bucks to take a seminar on how to free yourself from debt. It's like taking an anger management class from Mel Gibson, or a self-esteem seminar from John Calvin. I should have planted an orchard instead.

There are people in life who have no regrets. I'm not one of them, but it pays to have a sense of humor about such things. After all, I'm in good company: Achilles, Sisyphus, Tantalus, Adam. Kindred spirits all. And Moses too, whose job it was to lead his people across a wilderness that was psychological as much as it was geographical. He never made it into the Promised Land because he struck a rock with his staff instead of speaking to the rock. *Oops.* I propose a toast to all of them: Here's to the prophetic perfect tense, gents! Here's to journeys that never end, infinite digressions, incremental progress, and frequent fuckups along the road to freedom.

Lift your half-filled glasses, and drink up! Here's to being satisfied and not being satisfied.

If the *meantime* is the *not yet,* then what words help us grasp the *already*? Christians have, I suppose, eternity. Hindus have Nirvana. Australian aborigines have dreamtime. As concepts, I like dreamtime the best because it conjures up colors, sounds, smells, and tastes. It sounds more like story time, which appeals to a storyteller. It's hard, on the other hand, to get excited about nothingness, and the word *eternity* makes me think of being stuck in an endless church service in which I must listen to that dreadful stuff they call praise music. But regardless of the name for it, finding a doorway into the *already* is the tricky part. How do we get there? Death? Love? A proper understanding of subatomic physics? Psilocybin mushrooms?

Not long ago, I sat at my father's bedside during his last night on earth. He was reaching his final destination, after crossing the distance from cradle to grave. Some people have asked me if his death was peaceful. I can't answer that. I don't know what peaceful means to a dying person. His body fought for breath. His eyes didn't appear to see me. It was a hard night, and it leaves me with difficult memories. It went on for a long time, or for what I would call a long time. I have no idea how my father experienced the passage of time on that night; perhaps he was already somewhere else. I held his hand, and sang him hymns, and told family stories about hikes, his kids and grandkids, his wife, the places he loved. I talked about chopping wood and catching rainbow trout at Wheatfields Lake. I took him with me into the Grand Canyon. I told him what he meant to me, and how much I loved him, and why. I've been told that hearing is the last of the senses to fade away; I hope this is true, because I hope that he heard me.

Anyone who has been by the bedside of a dying person all through a long night knows what I mean when I say that he seemed outside of time. Or maybe outside of the meantime. Some would say that "he had one foot in heaven," or some such thing. I don't know what that means. There is no way for me to know what that means. Heaven is in the prophetic perfect tense, and I am in the meantime. Others might say that there is no mystery in this journey, his brain was just shutting down. What his last hours reminded me of is the last fifty yards of a 400-meter race when about all that is left in the consciousness is an almost automatic need to keep going, keep struggling against the limits of an exhausted body. Somewhere in that journey, time and space vanish. It is as if the body is a circle, and the spirit is a Koch snowflake inside of it.

We all have our own races to run, and we all have that last fifty yards. I'm not there yet. What will I do here in the meantime? Like Sisyphus, I'll roll the boulder again. I'll look for the damn keys every morning. Like Achilles, I'll keep assuming that my effort will get me somewhere. I'll pet the dogs and plant a garden. I'll keep running those pointless 400-meter dashes. I will love those whom I love, and occasionally I'll feel like they are an uncrossable distance away from me—but I'll love them no less for that. And like Adam, I'll keep my hand outstretched—waiting, waiting. For what? Freedom? Sanctification? Solvency? Enlightenment? The perfect wave? The perfect taco truck?

Yes. Such waiting is not passive; like prayer, it is actively attentive. I think both freedom and love come through paying attention, and together they unhinge us from the limitations of time and space. On my first date with the woman who is now my wife, she told me that she thought the point of life was learning how to love well. I thought it interesting that her answer was a process rather than a destination. Or maybe it's both—and we have *already and not yet* arrived. In either case, I liked her answer. It is as good an answer as I'm likely to get.

BIOGRAPHICAL NOTE

Mark Rozema was raised in the mountain town of Flagstaff, Arizona. His formative years were spent in the bed of a pickup truck, careening down dusty reservation roads, and exploring remote canyons with his dingo-Aussie mutt. Adulthood found him on farms, fishing boats, and fire lines, in group homes, and in classrooms. After leaving Arizona, he wandered through Utah, Alaska, and Montana, eventually landing in Washington, where he now tutors students at Edmonds Community College. He received an MFA from the University of Montana in 1990. His writing celebrates the ways in which identity is shaped by relationships to landscape, community, and family. His essays can be found in various journals, including *Flyway, Weber Studies, Isthmus, Under the Sun, Sport Literate,* and *Superstition Review.* He lives in Shoreline, Washington, with his wife, daughter, and two dogs.